LINEAR ALGEBRA
WITH
MAPLE® V

LINEAR ALGEBRA WITH *MAPLE® V*

Eugene W. Johnson
The University of Iowa

Brooks/Cole Publishing Company
Pacific Grove, California

Brooks/Cole Publishing Company
A Division of Wadsworth, Inc.

Printed in the United States of America

10 9 8 7 6 5 4 3 2 1

Library of Congress Cataloging in Publication Data
Johnson, Eugene W., [date]–
    Linear algebra with Maple V / Eugene W. Johnson.
        p.   cm. — (Brooks/Cole symbolic computation series)
    Includes index.
    ISBN 0-534-13069-0
    1. Algebras, Linear—Data processing.   2. Maple (Computer file)
I. Title.   II. Series.
QA185.D37J64   1993
512'.5'02855369—dc20   93-12881
                                                            CIP

Sponsoring Editor: *Jeremy Hayhurst*
Editorial Assistants: *Nancy Champlin* and *Elizabeth Barelli*
Production Coordinator: *Marlene Thom*
Manuscript Editor: *David Abel*
Cover Design: *Susan Haberkorn*
Typesetting: *Scratchgravel Publishing Services*
Printing and Binding: *Malloy Lithographing, Inc.*

To my wife, Sandy,
for her patience and support
through the many months of the writing
of this book

Preface

I began the present work before collaborating on the *Maple® V Flight Manual* (Ellis et al., Brooks/Cole, Pacific Grove, Calif., 1992), yet it is essentially an expansion and enhancement of the fourth chapter of that book. This work is both less and more advanced than the *Flight Manual*. The *Flight Manual* catalogues *Maple*'s linear algebra commands in greater depth and assumes more extensive knowledge of linear algebra on the part of the reader. On the other hand, this book contains significantly more mathematics, many more examples, and a fair collection of example applications. It also avoids the use of many of *Maple*'s powerful commands in favor of more elementary techniques.

I have had the pleasure of sharing ideas with a number of talented people in the course of this project; it is my hope that the reader will also find enjoyment in its use.

Acknowledgments

I would like to thank the following people from Brooks/Cole Publishing Company: Jeremy Hayhurst and Robert Evans for their devotion to *Maple* as an educational tool and for their cooperation and support in this project, and Nancy Champlin for her encouraging cheerfulness and assistance. I would also like to thank Marlene Thom for the many improvements she suggested to the manuscript.

The Symbolic Computation Group and Waterloo Maple Software have been of immense help. They are a dedicated, tireless, and talented bunch, and I have benefitted greatly, both directly and indirectly, from contact with each of the members. Particular thanks go to Keith Geddes, for his decision to modify *Maple V* to make it friendlier and more accessible to students, and for inviting me to participate with the group in a highly productive exchange of ideas; to Mike Monagan for his ideas and tireless efforts to expand and enhance the program; to Greg Fee for uncounted hours of programming, and for assisting me in *Maple* programming; to Benton Leong for coordinating my efforts with those of the group; and to George Labahn for stimulating conversation and help in understanding *Maple*. The list goes on to include Stan Devitt, Janet Cater, Blaire Madore, Katy Simonsen, and Lee Qiao, and others too numerous to mention.

Thanks also go to the many students at the University of Iowa who have participated in the development of this text by using it and sharing their impressions. They have acted as pioneers in the development of a new approach to teaching. Only time will demonstrate the importance of their efforts.

Finally, I wish to thank the following reviewers for their insightful comments: William Bauldry, Appalachian State University; Maurino Bautista, Rochester Institute of Technology; Benny Evans, Oklahoma State University; James L. Hartman, The College of Wooster; David R. Hill, Temple University; Barry Kirsch, Naval Air Warfare Center/Aircraft Division; Joseph Klerlein, Western Carolina University; Robert Lopez, Rose-Hulman Institute of Technology; John Mathews, California State University, Fullerton; Jeanette Palmiter, Portland State University; and Carol Scheftic, Carnegie-Mellon University.

Eugene W. Johnson
University of Iowa

Contents

3   Eigenspaces   86

LINEAR ALGEBRA
WITH
MAPLE® V

0 Introduction

Linear algebra is the primary tool for working with mathematical systems. The elements of such systems might be numbers, equations, functions, or other algebraic objects. Because such systems are required for the solution of problems in all scientific disciplines, linear algebra is one of the central topics in mathematics.

By collecting the related components of a problem into a system that can be dealt with as a single algebraic entity, an extremely important conceptual simplification is obtained. This simplification can often turn a confusing maze of information into a compact mathematical problem for which there is a straightforward, well-defined solution process. This is the appeal of linear algebra.

Unfortunately, even straightforward, well-defined solution processes are not necessarily either short or quick. But there now exist excellent computer programs that can assist dramatically by handling the routine calculations, freeing the user to concentrate on the strategy for solving a problem. This book is based on the use of one such system called *Maple*.

Maple® is a powerful computer program for doing mathematical computations. *Maple* "knows" virtually all standard mathematical functions and operations. Further, *Maple* plots graphs and can be "taught" things it did not originally know.

In some respects, *Maple* can be likened to a super-programmable graphing calculator. However, unlike most calculators, *Maple* is not restricted to performing its calculations with decimal approximations. It is quite capable of doing approximate calculations with "approximate numbers" if that is your choice. On the other hand, *Maple* can also do *exact* arithmetic with *exact* data—including unknowns and variables—as is typically done in the mathematics classroom.

Using *Maple*, you can relegate routine calculations to the computer without having to sacrifice total accuracy. This is no minor gain, as the cumulative effect of rounding errors in problems involving systems is serious enough to be substance for a separate course. (However, if you wish to use floating-point routines, *Maple* is also well equipped to assist you there.)

The breadth and flexibility of *Maple* can serve you well. The time you invest learning the program will pay dividends far beyond your study of linear algebra.

0.1 Getting Started with *Maple*

Maple is available for a large variety of computer systems, and the exact method of starting *Maple* will vary from system to system. I assume that you are familiar with the general principles of operating the computer on which *Maple* resides. Whatever the computer, *Maple* is launched in the same way as other applications on that system.

As a warm up, enter the examples in the "tour" (0.3) to get a feel for the way things work. You might also try a little experimenting on your own. There are three key points to keep in mind.

1. If you don't end a command with a semicolon (;), *Maple* will not report the result.

2. You tell *Maple* to *read* the command you have typed by pressing the appropriate key. This will probably be labeled **Enter** or **Return.** For example, on the Apollo Computer®, you can use either **Enter** or **Return.** On the Sun Computer®, only **Return** works. On the Macintosh®, only **Enter** works. Some experimentation on your part may be required. If there is nobody around who can tell you what works, just go ahead and try **Enter** or **Return** and see what happens. If *Maple* seems to have paid no attention, chances are you need to use a different key.

3. *If Maple totally ignores your commands, reread 1 and 2.* If *Maple* is reading your commands but simply does not understand them, it will normally respond with an error message.

0.2 Editing, Saving, and Retrieving Your Work

Some file-handling commands provided by *Maple* are common across all systems. However, most systems provide additional capabilities based on their own hardware and operating systems. Editing operations are also quite system specific.

Specific, system-dependent information is available in the *Maple Language Reference Manual.*

0.3 An Introductory Tour of *Maple*

Maple is no more difficult to operate than a pocket calculator. Throughout this tour, commands entered by the user are shown in Courier type, followed by *Maple*'s response. The exact form of the response may vary from that shown, depending on your operating system and release of *Maple V*. The marginal notes contain discussions of the *Maple* sessions.

0.3.1   Arithmetic

Standard Notation	Maple Notation
$x + y$	x + y
$x - y$	x - y
xy	x * y
x/y	x / y
x^y	x ^ y
	x**y

Unlike most calculators and computer programs, *Maple* has an "exact" mode.

Use the standard plus sign (+) for addition. This computes the sum $\frac{1}{3} + \frac{4}{5}$. Maple's response always begins on a new line.

• `1/3 + 4/5;`

$$\frac{17}{15}$$

Use the minus sign (–) for subtraction. This computes the difference $\frac{34}{55} - \frac{114}{27}$.

• `34/55 - 114/27;`

$$\frac{-1784}{495}$$

Use the asterisk (*) for multiplication. This computes the product $\frac{24}{47} \times \frac{94}{96}$.

• `24/47 * 94/96;`

$$\frac{47}{54}$$

Use the standard forward slash (/) for division as well as for fractions.

• `56/28;`

$$2$$

Use the caret symbol (^) to denote exponents. This gives 2^{64}. (You can also use the double asterisk (**) instead.)

• `2^64;`

$$18446744073709551616$$

Maple can also perform exact calculations with some special numbers and virtually all standard mathematical functions.

*This computes the product
$\sqrt{3}\sqrt{4}$. Note that Maple
prints the result with a
space to denote the product
and uses $3^{1/2}$ in place of
$\sqrt{3}$.*

- `sqrt(3) * sqrt(4);`

$$2\sqrt{3}$$

*Maple uses I for $\sqrt{-1}$. This
computes I^2.*

- `I^2;`

$$-1$$

*This demonstrates Maple's
accurate calculation of the
log and exponential func-
tions.*

- `log(exp(3/5));`

$$\frac{3}{5}$$

When you use decimal notation, *Maple* reacts like a standard calculator with ten digits of precision, rounding errors and all; this is *Maple*'s "approximate" mode.

*This computes a decimal
approximation of $\frac{1}{3} + \frac{6}{7}$.
Note the rounding error.*

- `.3333333333 + .8571428571;`

$$1.190476190$$

*This computes an approxi-
mation of $\sqrt{2}$.*

- `sqrt(2.0);`

$$1.414213562$$

*This squares the approxima-
tion of $\sqrt{2}$.*

- `sqrt(2.0)^2;`

$$1.999999999$$

*This computes a decimal
approximation of 2^{64}.
Compare this to the exact
answer obtained earlier.*

- `2.0^64;`

$$.1844674407 \ 10^{20}$$

0.3.2 Prompts

When *Maple* is ready for you to enter a command, most versions display a *prompt*. A prompt is simply an indicator that *Maple* is waiting for you to give it an instruction. The system on which this manuscript was prepared uses a large dot (•) for its primary prompt; if you have been wondering why the *Maple* commands in the preceding examples all have a large dot in front of them, you now know the reason. *Maple* also uses a secondary prompt to tell the user that it is waiting for the *completion* of an instruction.

Maple's prompts are system dependent, so the primary or secondary prompts on your system may differ from those shown here. Many systems use ">" for both the primary and secondary prompt. On some systems, the prompts can be modified by the user.

This book uses "•" for the primary prompt and "»" for the secondary prompt.

0.3.3   The Terminators in *Maple*

Instructions to *Maple* can extend over more than one line. To make this possible, it is necessary to use a terminator to signal *Maple* at the end of each instruction. The semicolon (;) serves this function.[1] As a consequence of using a terminator, more than one command can be entered on one line.

Each *Maple* instruction must end with a semicolon (;). Otherwise, *Maple* will not respond with an answer.

You can spread one command over several lines. Here, the secondary prompt (») shows a command is continuing.

```
• 1
» +
» 2
» ;
```
$$3$$

You can also place more than one command on one line.

```
• 1+2;  2/3-3/5;
```
$$3$$

$$\frac{1}{15}$$

In both cases, you use the semicolon to indicate the end of a command.

---

[1]It is also possible to terminate a command with the colon (:). The colon is *Maple*'s "silent" terminator. When it is used, output is (usually) suppressed.

0.3.4 Getting Help

Maple has an extensive help system; help is available for virtually any topic. To get help, you can use either of two styles: `?topic` or `help(`*topic*`);`.

Help is even available on getting help.

- `?help`

(Only a small corner of the help screen is shown here.)

Note that a semicolon is not required when help is called in this way.

```
FUNCTION:   Help - description of syntax, datatypes

CALLING SEQUENCE:

 ?topic   or   ?topic,subtopic   or   ?topic[subtopic]
 help(topic)   or   help(topic,subtopic) or help(top

SYNOPSIS:
        ?intro        introduction to Maple
        ?library      Maple library functions and proce
        ?index        list of all help categories
```

0.3.5 Ditto, Ditto, Ditto

Maple uses the ditto (also known as double quotes (")) to refer to the result of the previous calculation. Similarly, the double ditto (" ") refers to the result immediately preceding the immediately preceding result. The triple ditto (" " ") is also implemented, but that is as far as it goes.

```
"       The result of the immediately preceding calculation.
" "     The result immediately preceding ".
" " "   The result immediately preceding " ".
```

After this calculation, 5 is the result of the immediately preceding calculation.

- `2+3;`

                5

This subtracts 12 from 5, the result of the immediately preceding calculation .

- `" - 12;`

                −7

This subtracts −7 from 5: −7 is the result of immediately preceding calculation and 5 is the result immediately preceding that.

- `" " - ";`

                12

This computes the product 5*(−7+12): " " " refers to 5, " " refers to −7 and " refers to 12.

- `" " " * ( " " + " );`

    25

0.3.6 Built-in Functions and Constants

Maple has an extensive library of built-in mathematical functions. Most are used as they would normally be written on paper. For a list of the functions known to *Maple* in its start-up state, type `?inifcns` in a *Maple* session. *Maple* also knows the standard mathematical constants e, π and i ($= \sqrt{-1}$).

Standard Notation	*Maple* Notation[2]
e	`exp(1)`
π	`Pi`
i	`I`
	`sqrt(-1)`

*Maple recognizes the mathematical constant **e** as* exp(1).

- `ln(exp(1));`

    1

Maple is also aware of the number π.

- `sin(Pi);`

    0

Maple is aware of i ($= \sqrt{-1}$) as I.

- `I^2;`

    −1

0.3.7 Approximate Solutions

In some cases exact answers are unobtainable; in others, the expression of an answer in exact form is so complicated that a decimal approximation is more desirable. Any numeric expression can be converted to a floating-point approximation in *Maple* by means of the `evalf` command. If desired, you can also specify the number of decimal digits.

Use evalf *to get a decimal approximation.*

- `evalf(Pi);`

    3.141592654

---

[2]This is the initial setup of *Maple V*. However, the symbol "I" can be used for another purpose if desired.

Maple's default decimal precision is ten, but you can increase or decrease it by resetting Digits. *Once reset, the new setting remains active until changed or until Maple is restarted.*

- Digits:=3;

$$Digits := 3$$

- evalf(Pi-22/7);

$$0$$

This resets Digits *to its initial value of* 10.

- Digits:=10;

$$Digits := 10$$

You can also specify the number of digits for a particular calculation without changing Digits. *Note Maple's use of the backslash (\\) to indicate continuation of the output.*

- evalf(Pi,500);

3.14159265358979323846264338327950288419716939\\
37510582097494459230781640628620899862803489\\
25342117067982148086513282306647093844609556\\
05822317253594081284811174502841027019385211\\
10555964462294895493038196442881097566593344\\
46128475648233786783165271201909145648566923\\
46034861045432664821339360726024914127372445\\
58700660631558817488152092096282925409171536\\
43678925903600113305305488204665213841469519\\
41511609433057270365759591953092186117381932\\
61179310511854807446237996274956735185885752\\
7248912279381830119491

0.3.8   Assigning Names

Any *Maple* expression—numerical, symbolic, or otherwise—can be assigned a name in *Maple* by using the assignment operator "colon equal" (:=). Once a name is assigned to an expression, the name can be used any time you want to refer to the expression. This greatly expands the type of functionality provided by the ditto marks, but it does rely on you to implement it.

Here the number $119 \times (476 + 23!)$ *is assigned the name "n".*

- n:=119*(476 + 23!);

$$n := 3076389991927312220216644$$

Here the number $12^{23} + 1936$ *is assigned the name "d".*

- d:=12^23+1936;

$$d := 6624737266949237011122064$$

Here the names "n" and "d" are used to calculate the quotient $\frac{n}{d}$, which is assigned the name q. Note the simplification.

- q:=n/d;

$$q := \frac{109871071140261150722023}{236597759533901321825788}$$

Names you assign can be used in conjunction with ditto marks. Unlike the dittos, the names you assign will retain the same values until you change them.

- " /n;

$$\frac{1}{662473726694923701122064}$$

0.3.9   Unassigning Names

In Section 0.3.8, the variables *n, d,* and *q* were assigned values and hence became constants. *Maple* also provides an easy way of "unassigning" variables, which involves forcing an assigned name to return its unassigned value—that is, itself. This is done with single quotes.[3]

If, for some reason, you wish to use an assigned name and not have Maple evaluate it as assigned, you use single forward quotes (') around the name. (Recall that d was assigned the value $12^{23} + 1936$ in the previous section.)

- 'd';

$$d$$

You unassign an assigned name or variable by reassigning it to its unassigned value.

This unassigns d by assigning it the value 'd'.

- d:='d';

$$d := d$$

Note that the variable d now evaluates to itself.

- d;

$$d$$

Note that once a variable is unassigned, it can be used as if it had never been assigned.

---

[3]Alternatively, you can use the command d:=evaln(d); for the same purpose.

0.3.10   Extending *Maple*

When you assign a name in *Maple*, you extend the domain of things known to the program, albeit in a rather minor fashion. However, more substantial extensions are possible. In particular, *Maple* allows you to extend it by defining new functions.

Although *Maple* has an extensive library of built-in functions, it will not have every function you might want. For example, simple functions such as $f(x) = x^2 + 1$ are not built in.

A function such as $f(x) = x^2 + 1$ is called an expression-based function, because its definition involves evaluation of the same expression regardless of the value of x. Compare this with the function

$$g(x) = \begin{cases} x^2 \text{ if } x < 2 \\ x \text{ otherwise} \end{cases}$$

where the rule applied to x depends on the value of x.

Maple has an easy way for you to define new expression-based functions. Because of the notation, functions defined in this way are called arrow-style functions.

This defines the function $f(x)$ = $x^2 + 1$ and evaluates it at $x = -1$ and at $x = 2$. The arrow is created by combining the minus and greater-than signs (–>).

- `f:=x->x^2+1;`

$$f := x \rightarrow x^2 + 1$$

- `f(-1);`

$$2$$

- `f(2);`

$$5$$

Functions that are not based on a single expression can be defined as *procedures.*

This defines the function

$$f(x) = \begin{cases} x^2 \text{ if } x < 2 \\ x \text{ otherwise} \end{cases}.$$

Functions defined by this method are called "proc functions."

- `f:=proc(x)`
- » `if x<2 then x^2`
- » `else x`
- » `fi;`
- » `end;`

`f := proc (x) if x < 2 then x^2 else x fi end`

Note the `proc...end` and `if...fi` pairings in the definition of *f.* The end signals *Maple* that the procedure definition is complete, and the `fi` signals that the `if...then...` construction is complete.

Here, the newly defined function f is applied to –1 and to 2.

- `f(-1);`

$$1$$

- `f(2);`

$$2$$

The "proc style" of definition can also be used for expression-based functions.

0.3.11 Symbolic Calculations with *Maple*

Maple can work with undefined symbols (e.g., unknowns and variables) using general rules of algebra: It treats expressions involving unassigned names as rational expressions in which the unassigned names are the variables.

This is the instruction for Maple to "compute"

$$\frac{x(x + x - y - x)}{x}.$$

Note that Maple cancels the x terms; the two rational expressions are equal, but the functions they define are not.

- `x*(x+x-y-x)/x;`

$$x - y$$

This is the command for Maple to factor the polynomial $x^4 - 12x^3 + 54x^2 - 108x + 81$.

- `factor(x^4-12*x^3+54*x^2-108*x+81);`

$$(x - 3)^4$$

This is the command for Maple to expand the polynomial $(x + 1)(x - 1)^3$.

- `expand((x+1)*(x-1)^3);`

$$x^4 + 2x^3 - 2x - 1$$

- `x^3-x+x^5`

$$x^3 - x + x^5$$

You can use the `sort` *command to put the terms of the polynomial into their natural order.*

- `sort(x^3-x+x^5);`

$$x^5 + x^3 - x$$

Here, Maple's ability to work with named quantities is used effectively in combination with its ability to work with symbolic quantities; recall that feet² is the standard scientific abbreviation for square feet.

- `height:=23*feet;`

$$height := 23\,feet$$

- `width:=14*feet;`

$$width := 14\,feet$$

- `area:=height*width;`

$$area := 322\,feet^2$$

0.3.12   Equations

In *Maple*, an equation consists of two expressions with an equal sign (=) between them.

Equations can be multiplied and manipulated using the standard "equals to equals" approach, as well as built-in commands. For example, the following session solves the simple linear equation $2x + 3 = 5$ for x. (Note the important distinction between ":=" and "=". The first assigns a value to a variable or expression; the latter defines an equation. The equation is named in the example to help point out the difference between ":=" and "=".)

This defines the equation.

- `eqn:=2*x+3=5;`

$$eqn := 2x + 3 = 5$$

This subtracts the equation $3 = 3$ from the equation $2x + 3 = 5$ as a first step in isolating x.

- `eqn-(3=3);`

$$2x = 2$$

This completes the isolation of x.

- `" * 1/2;`

$$x = 1$$

Though it may occasionally be amusing to manipulate equations manually to solve them, often you will want to let *Maple* take care of such details. *Maple* has routines for solving many sorts of equations. Its most basic equation solver is simply called `solve`.

The `solve` command returns exact solutions: It returns all that it finds, but it may not always find all possible solutions, and it sometimes reports extraneous solutions.

Here the solve *command solves the equation* $2x + 3 = 5$ *for x.*

- solve(2*x+3=5,{x});

$$\{x = 1\}$$

Here solve *is used to find the roots of a quadratic equation. Maple reports both solutions.*

- solve(x^2-3*x+1=0,{x});

$$\left\{x = \frac{3}{2} + \frac{1}{2}\sqrt{5}\right\}, \left\{x = \frac{3}{2} - \frac{1}{2}\sqrt{5}\right\}$$

You can use solve *without placing either the equation(s) or the variables in set braces; the form of the result is slightly different.*

- solve(x^2-3*x+1=0,x);

$$\frac{3}{2} + \frac{1}{2}\sqrt{5}, \frac{3}{2} - \frac{1}{2}\sqrt{5}$$

Here, solve *is used to solve the equation* $\sin(x) = 0$ *for x. Only the value* 0 *is returned.*

- solve(sin(x)=0,x);

$$0$$

In this case, solve *returns an exact answer that begs the question. (There are no formulas for solutions of sixth degree polynomials.)*

- solve(x^6-x-1=0,x);

$$\text{RootOf}(\_Z^6 - \_Z - 1)$$

Not all solutions can be expressed in a satisfactory exact form. Hence, in some cases, you may want to settle for—or even prefer—a decimal approximation of the exact solution. You can use fsolve for this.

Use fsolve *to obtain an approximate solution.*

- fsolve(x^6-x-1=0,x);

$$-.7780895987, 1.134724138$$

In this case, one would guess that there are additional complex solutions. If you wish fsolve to find complex as well as real solutions, you can use the optional argument complex.

You can use fsolve *to obtain complex solutions as well.*

- fsolve(x^6-x-1=0,x,complex);

$$-.7780895987, -.6293724285 - .7357559530\,I,$$
$$-.6293724285 + .7357559530\,I,$$
$$.4510551586 - 1.002364572\,I,$$
$$.4510551586 + 1.002364572\,I, 1.134724138$$

For a complete description of the options that can be used with fsolve, see the *Maple* help page on fsolve (type ?fsolve in a *Maple* session).

0.3.13   Calculus with *Maple*

If you have not used *Maple* before, you may be surprised by its ability to solve calculus problems. There are many interesting problems that involve both calculus and linear algebra.

This is the Maple equivalent of $\frac{d}{dx}\sin(x)$.

- diff(sin(x),x);

$$\cos(x)$$

This computes the second derivative of $\sin(x)$.

- diff(sin(x),x$2);

$$-\sin(x)$$

This is the Maple equivalent of f' for $f = \sin$.

- D(sin);

$$\cos$$

This is the Maple equivalent of f'' for $f = \sin$.

- (D@@2)(sin);

$$-\sin$$

This is the Maple equivalent of $\int \cos(x)dx$.

- int(cos(x),x);

$$\sin(x)$$

Here is an example that shows a bit more of Maple's power.

- int(1/(x^3+1),x);

$$\frac{1}{3}\ln(x+1)-\frac{1}{6}\ln(x^2-x+1)+\frac{1}{3}\sqrt{3}\arctan\left(\frac{1}{3}(2x-1)\sqrt{3}\right)$$

This evaluates the definite integral of $\frac{1}{x}$ from e to e^2.

- int(1/x,x=exp(1)..exp(2));

$$1$$

If you ever need to solve differential equations, you will appreciate *Maple*'s dsolve command.

This solves the differential equation $f''(x) = f(x)$. Here, _C1 and _C2 are arbitrary constants.

- dsolve(diff(f(x),x$2)- f(x)= 0, f(x));

$$f(x) = \_C1\,e^x + \_C2\,e^{-x}$$

This solves the initial value problem
$f'(x) = f(x), f(0) = 3.$

- dsolve({diff(f(x),x)- f(x)=0,f(0)=3},
» f(x));

$$f(x) = 3e^x$$

0.3.14   Graphing Functions with *Maple*

It is often helpful to get a picture of the problem you are trying to solve. *Maple* can assist in this regard by drawing graphs of functions.

This is the command to generate the graph of the expression $y = x^3 - x + 1.$

- plot(x^3-x+1,x=-10..10);

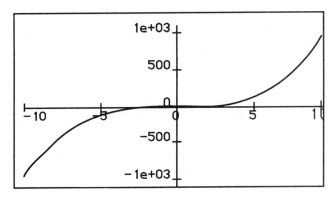

Figure 0.1 $y = x^3 - x + 1$

This is the command to graph the same equation on the interval [–2,2]. *Notice that this clarifies some of the key features of the graph.*

- plot(x^3-x+1,x=-2..2);

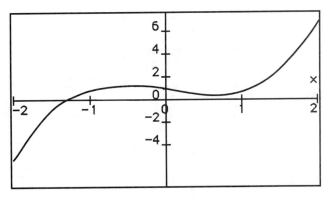

Figure 0.2 $y = x^3 - x + 1, -2 \le x \le 2$

This is the command to generate a 3-dimensional plot of $z = \sin(x) + \cos(y)$ for x and y in $[-\pi, \pi]$.

```
• plot3d(sin(x)+cos(y),x=-Pi..Pi,
» y=-Pi..Pi);
```

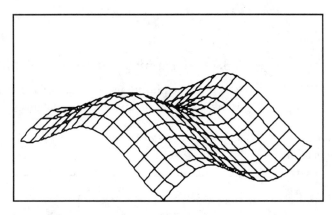

Figure 0.3 $z = \sin(x) + \cos(y)$

0.3.15   Other Types of *Maple* Objects

Maple can work with a large variety of object types; functions, symbols, exact numbers, decimal numbers, graphs, and equations are just a few. Some other important types of objects that *Maple* can use are illustrated in the following examples.

Here, sets are used. (They were used above with the solve *command.) Sets are created with curly braces ("{" and "}").*

```
• Set1:={2*x-3,3*y-2,1,2};
```

$$Set1 := \{1, 2, 2x - 3, 3y - 2\}$$

```
• Set2:={3*z-5,7};
```

$$Set2 := \{7, 3z - 5\}$$

Use union *for union and* intersect *for intersection.*

```
• Set1 union Set2;
```

$$\{1, 2, 7, 2x - 3, 3y - 2, 3z - 5\}$$

{} denotes the empty set.

```
• Set1 intersect Set2;
```

$$\{\}$$

Here, x_1, x_2, x_3 and x_2, x_3, x_4 are sequences.

```
• Seq1:=x1,x2,x3;
```

$$Seq1 := x1,x2,x3$$

The empty sequence is denoted NULL.

- `Seq2:=x2,x3,x4;`

$$Seq2 := x2,x3,x4$$

You can append one sequence to the end of another to make one longer sequence.

- `Seq3:=Seq1,Seq2;`

$$Seq3 := x1, x2, x3, x2, x3, x4$$

You form a set from a sequence by enclosing it in curly braces.[4]

- `Set3:={Seq3};`

$$Set3 := \{x4, x1, x2, x3\}$$

Here, [sin, cos, tan] *is a list.*

- `List:=[sin,cos;tan];`

$$List := [sin,cos,tan]$$

`S[i]` *denotes the ith element of a list or set or sequence S.*

- `Seq1[2];`

$$x2$$

- `List[1];`

$$sin$$

The op *of a list or set is the sequence of elements in it (up to the order of the elements in the case of sets).*[5]

- `op(List);`

$$sin, cos, tan$$

- `op(Set3);`

$$x4, x1, x2, x3$$

You can use nops *to count the number of elements in a list or set.*

- `nops(List);`

$$3$$

- `nops(Set1 union Set2);`

$$6$$

---

[4]Note that Maple may not keep the elements of the set in the order they have in the sequence.
[5]Sets are order independent.

When a list or array of functions is applied to a number or symbol, each of the functions is applied.

- `List(Pi);`

$$[0, -1, 0]$$

Here, A is a matrix— a two-dimensional array. Note that the argument is a list of lists. The inner lists are the rows of the matrix.[6]

- `A:=linalg[matrix]([[1,2],[3,4]]);`

$$A := \begin{bmatrix} 1 & 2 \\ 3 & 4 \end{bmatrix}$$

A[i,j] denotes the entry in the ith row and jth column of the matrix A.

- `A[1,2];`

$$2$$

0.3.16 Substitution

In mathematics, it is frequently desirable to substitute one quantity for another, perhaps to simplify an expression, perhaps for other reasons—such as to obtain a definite integral from an antiderivative.

The subs *command is used to substitute one quantity for another.*

- `F:=int(x^2-1,x);`

$$F := \frac{1}{3}x^3 - x$$

This gives

$$\int_a^b (x^2 - 1)dx.[7]$$

- `subs(x=b,F)-subs(x=a,F);`

$$\frac{1}{3}b^3 - b - \frac{1}{3}a^3 + a$$

0.3.17 Automating Repetitive Procedures: Loops

It is often necessary to repeat an operation on a sequence of objects. Loops provide the necessary mechanism. *Maple* provides two forms of the "for" loop. One form is as follows:

```
for index from start by  inc  to finish  while
conditional
      do
                first_thing_to_do;
                second_thing_to_do;
```

---

[6]If the matrix is formed following the command `with(linalg);` then the shorter form `matrix(..);` can be used.
[7]This integral can also be evaluated with the single command `int(x^2-1,x=a..b);`.

```
                    .
                    .
        last_thing_to_do;
    od;
```

where *index* is a counter (*i, j, m,* and *n* are common choices), *start* is the beginning value of *index*, and *inc* is the amount by which *index* is incremented on each pass through the loop. The loop will terminate (and not execute the list of things to be done) the first time *index* exceeds *finish* or *conditional* evaluates to false. The "from *start* " and "by *inc* " clauses are optional; if they are omitted, the value 1 is assumed in each case. The "to *finish*" and "while *conditional*" clauses are also optional, but if you leave both out the loop will run forever unless other provisions are made. Use ?do in a *Maple* session for more information on other options with do...od.

A second form of the "for" loop is given by the following.

```
for index in list while conditional
    do
            first_thing_to_do;
            second_thing_to_do;
                    .
                    .
            last_thing_to_do;
    od;
```

where *index* is a variable (*i, j, m,* and *n* are common choices) and *list* is a list of values to be assumed in turn by *index* (these values need not be numerical). The loop will terminate (and not execute the list of things remaining to be done) when *list* is exhausted or *conditional* evaluates to false. The "while *conditional*" clause is optional.

A special note regarding loops: the counter is left with a value at the end of a loop. This means you will frequently need to unassign names of variables you have used as counters. (The exact value depends on the exact form of the loop used.)

Consider the following simple example.

This simple loop merely prints each of the first three natural numbers. In this case, the counter is i, start and inc are 1 by default, and finish is 3. The counter is left with the value 4.

```
• for i to 3
» do
»   print(i);
» od;
                1
                2
                3

• i;
                4
```

This unassigns the variable i for later use.

- `i:='i';`

$$i := i$$

0.3.18   Generating Sequences, Sums, and Products

Maple has special functions for generating sequences, sums, and products from formulas.

This generates the sequence of factorials of the first ten natural numbers. The seq *commend can use an assigned counter, so it is not necessary to first execute the command* i:='i';.

- `seq(i!,i=1..10);`

1, 2, 6, 24, 120, 720, 5040, 40320, 362880, 3628800

This unassigns i and computes the sum $\sum_{i=1}^{10} i!$ *of the factorials of the first ten natural numbers. (The use of i as a counter in the* seq *command left it with a value assigned; the* sum *command cannot use an assigned counter.)*

- `i:='i';`

$$i := i$$

- `sum(i!,i=1..10);`

4037913

This gives the product $\prod_{i=1}^{10} 2i$ *of the first ten even natural numbers. (The use of i as a counter with* sum *did not leave it with an assigned value. However, you may want to routinely unassign counter variables before using them with* sum *or* product.)

- `i:='i';`

$$i := i$$

- `product(2*i,i=1..10);`

3715891200

Both a loop and the seq command will leave the counter with a value. Both can also use counters with assigned values. On the other hand, neither sum nor product will leave the counter with a value, nor will they accept a counter with a value. You may want to develop the habit of unassigning the counter variable before using `sum` or `product`; this text will adopt this convention.

Here is an example of what happens if you used an assigned variable as a counter with `sum` or `product`.

This assigns i the value 3 and then attempts to use i as a counter in product *and* sum.

- `i:=3;`

$$i := 3$$

These responses are called "error messages."

- `product(i,i=1..10);`
`Error, (in product) product variable previously`
`assigned, second argument evaluates to 3 = 1..10`

- `sum(i,i=1..5);`
`Error, (in sum) summation variable previously`
`assigned, second argument evaluates to`
`3 = 1 .. 5`

0.3.19 Aliases and Macros

Mathematics is full of special abbreviations and notations, many of them a matter of personal choice. The `alias` command lets you use your preferred notation in some cases. For example, you might prefer to use the abbreviation `prod` for the `product` command or `e` for `exp(1)`. The procedure for doing so is demonstrated in the following.

This "aliases" prod *to* product *and* e *to* exp(1). *Note that Maple lists all active aliases.*

- `alias(prod=product, e=exp(1));`

$$I, prod, e$$

Now both you and Maple can use prod *and* e *in place of* product *and* exp(1) —*you can still use the original names if you wish. (The symbol i is unassigned here as a matter of course preparatory to using it with* prod, *now another name for* prod- uct.)

- `i:='i';`

$$i := i$$

- `prod(i,i=1..5);`

$$120$$

- `int(1/x,x=1..e);`

$$1$$

- `exp(1);`

$$e$$

This "unaliases prod. *(The system is initially configured with I aliased to $\sqrt{-1}$.)*

- alias(prod=prod);

$$I$$

Note that Maple is now completely unaware of prod.

- prod(i,i=1..5);

$$\mathrm{prod}(i, i = 1 .. 5)$$

- exp(1);

$$e$$

In addition to the alias facility, *Maple* provides a macro facility. The following is an example of the use of a macro. Assume that you are computing a number of polynomial expressions and that you want to use the simplify command on each of them.

This defines SS *as a macro for* simplify("). *Note that there is no output from Maple.*

- macro(SS=simplify("));

You can now use SS any time in place of simplify(").

This defines a rational expression.

- i:='i';

$$i := i$$

- p:=product((x^i-1)/(x-1),i=1..3);

$$p := \frac{(x^2 - 1)(x^3 - 1)}{(x - 1)^2}$$

This simplifies the expression.

- SS;

$$(x + 1)(x^2 + x + 1)$$

You undefine a macro by redefining it to be itself.

- macro(SS=SS);

There is some similarity between an alias and a macro, but there are important differences as well. For example, if SS had been used as an alias for simplify("), rather than as a macro, the result of using the "command" SS on the preceding *Maple* output would simply have been SS.

This defines SS *as an alias for the command* simplify("").

- alias(SS=simplify(""));

$$I, SS$$

This reinstates p as the previous result.

- p;

$$\frac{(x^2 - 1)(x^3 - 1)}{(x - 1)^2}$$

Applying the alias SS *has no effect on p.*

- SS;

$$SS$$

The primary purpose of the macro facility is to allow the user to define keyboard shortcuts. Use ?alias and ?macro for a more complete discussion.

0.3.20 Simplification and Evaluation

In Section 0.3.19, the simplify command was used to force cancellation of a common factor in the numerator and denominator of a quotient. As the example demonstrated, *Maple* does not always reduce expressions to their simplest form. There are a number of reasons for this: one is that time is saved when simplification is not required; another is that sometimes it is not clear how to proceed or what is desired.

Because expressions are not always put in a simplified or standard form, *Maple* has a number of special-purpose commands that can be used to change the form of an answer. You have already seen simplify used, as well as evalf. Here is a list of additional commands that you may find particularly useful.

evalc	evaluate as a complex number (i.e., to the form $a + bi$)
evalm	evaluate as a matrix (or vector)
evaln	evaluate as a name
evalf	evaluate as a floating-point number
expand	expand a polynomial expression
factor	factor a polynomial expression
normal	put a quotient of polynomials into the form numerator/ denominator, both factored and with no common factors
simplify	a general-purpose simplifier

Use the help system for more detailed information.

0.3.21 Quitting a *Maple* Session

You end a session with the quit *command.*

- quit;

This tour has touched on only the basic capabilities of *Maple*. For further introductory reading of a general nature, you are referred to the *First Leaves* tutorial.[8] For more technical information, consult the *Maple V Language Reference Manual*[9] and the *Maple V Library Reference Manual*.[10]

EXERCISES

Use the examples in the tour and the help system to guide you in the following exercises.

1. a. Compute the sum s and product p of the first 20 odd integers. (Note that an odd integer is of the form $2i + 1$.)
   b. Compute the quotient s/p and the power p^s. (You will have to wait for *Maple* to complete the latter calculation.)
   c. Try to compute s^p.
   d. Use forward quotes to unassign the variables s and p.

2. Differentiate and integrate the quotient $\dfrac{1}{(x^2 + 1)^2}$.

3. Plot the function $\dfrac{1}{(x^2 + 1)^2}$ on the interval $[-5,5]$.

4. By experimentation, determine the smallest integer n for which $n! > 10^n$. (You may be able to put loops to good use here.)

5. The function $\text{GAMMA}(x) = \displaystyle\int_0^\infty e^{-t}t^{x-1}dt$ is a built-in *Maple* function.

   Compare $\text{GAMMA}(n)$ to $n!$ for several values of n. What do you guess is the relation between the two? Use a loop to verify your guess for $n = 1 \dots 50$.

6. a. Assign the value 20! to the variable `fact`.
   b. Assign the number of seconds in a billion years to the variable `time`.
   c. Compute the ratio `fact/time`.
   d. Use either forward quotes or the `evaln` command to unassign the variables `fact` and `time`.

7. Define the function $f(x) = x^3 - 3x + 1124$ and evaluate it at $x = -1234$, -123, -12, 0, 12, 123, 1234.

8. Define the function $g(x) = \dfrac{x^3 - x + 2}{x^5 - 3x + 27}$ and graph it using the *Maple* `plot` command.

---

[8]*First Leaves,* Char et al. (New York: Springer-Verlag, 1992).
[9]*Maple V Language Reference Manual,* Char et al. (New York: Springer-Verlag, 1991).
[10]*Maple V Library Reference Manual,* Char et al. (New York: Springer-Verlag, 1991).

9. Use the `plot3d` command to plot the graph of the expression 4 sin(4*x*) + 10 cos(*y*), for *x* = −π ... π and *y* = −π ... π. (Recall that π is denoted Pi in *Maple*.)

10. If you are so inclined, you can use the `alias` command for some skullduggery. Alias `sum` to `product` and issue the command `sum(i,i=0..5);`. Be sure to unalias `sum` so you don't fall victim to your dirty deed! (Fortunately, aliases, like virtually all the things you do in a *Maple* session, are forgotten when the session is ended.)

1 Matrices and Linear Systems

Beginning in this chapter, *Maple*'s responses to commands are not necessarily shown. Comments regarding the output follow or replace the actual output. The commands are intended to be entered as shown; you can then observe *Maple*'s response interactively. The keywords in square brackets immediately following a section head are *Maple* commands used for the first time in that section.

1.1 The Linear Algebra Package
[with, linalg]

Maple has a number of special-purpose "packages" that must be loaded before they can be used. The linear algebra package, called `linalg`, contains the standard functions of linear algebra as well as a number of special-purpose functions.

The first order of business is to load the `linalg` *package using Maple's* `with` *command.*

- `with(linalg);`
The names of the commands and functions that are loaded are listed on the screen. This *must* be done at the beginning of each session or if variables are cleared (which is not possible with some versions of *Maple*).

You can use Maple's help system at any time to review the names of the `linalg` *functions.*

- `?linalg`
Don't be surprised if you are unfamiliar with many of the function names. Linear algebra has many specialized functions.

1.2 Gaussian Elimination and Row Reduction
[matrix, augment]

The great philosopher and mathematician René Descartes advocated a simple two-step strategy for the solution of problems:

1. break the problem into solvable components;
2. solve the components.

In linear algebra, a surprising number of problems can be broken into components that require the solution of a system of linear equations, giving this rather elementary operation a position of special prominence. Solving systems of linear equations is a straightforward but time-consuming and error-prone task for which *Maple* can be very helpful.

A common strategy for solving a system of linear equations such as

$$a_{11}x_1 + a_{12}x_2 + \cdots + a_{1n}x_n = b_1$$
$$a_{21}x_1 + a_{22}x_2 + \cdots + a_{2n}x_n = b_2$$
$$\vdots$$
$$a_{m1}x_1 + a_{m2}x_2 + \cdots + a_{mn}x_n = b_m$$

is to augment the coefficient matrix $A = [a_{ij}]$ by the matrix $B = [b_i]$ of constants to form the augmented matrix of the system

$$[A, B] = \begin{bmatrix} a_{11} & a_{12} & \cdot & \cdot & \cdot & a_{1n} & b_1 \\ a_{21} & a_{22} & \cdot & \cdot & \cdot & a_{2n} & b_2 \\ & & & \cdot & & & \\ & & & \cdot & & & \\ a_{m1} & a_{m2} & \cdot & \cdot & \cdot & a_{mn} & b_m \end{bmatrix}$$

and then use Gaussian elimination (that is, row reduction) and back-substitution to obtain the solution.

You can follow this same strategy in *Maple*. For example, given the linear system

$$2x_1 + x_2 \quad + 4x_3 \quad = \frac{41}{4}$$
$$3x_1 + \frac{3}{2}x_2 + \frac{34}{5}x_3 = \frac{41}{12}$$
$$\frac{2}{3}x_2 + 5x_3 \quad = \frac{35}{4}$$

you can form the augmented matrix of the system as follows.

Define the coefficient matrix with the matrix *command.*

- `A:=matrix(`
» `[[2,1,4],`
» `[3,3/2,34/5],`
» `[0,2/3,5]]);`

Actually, you could enter all (or any part) of this on one line, but this arrangement makes it easier to see the rows.

Define the matrix B of constants.

- `B:=matrix([[41/4],[41/12],[35/4]]);`

In this case, it is convenient to put all the entries on one line. Follow your own preference.

Form the augmented matrix [A,B] using the augment *command.*[1]

- `A_B:=augment(A,B);`

The notation A_B for $[A,B]$ is a compromise. (The underscore character (_) is a shifted hyphen). $[A,B]$ is a data structure (a list) in *Maple*, and *Maple* does not permit data structures to be used as names. An attempt to use $[A,B]$ as a name results in the error message, "Error, Illegal use of an object as a name."[2]

1.2.1 Manual Row Reduction
[addrow, mulrow, swaprow, pivot]

You can step through the Gaussian elimination procedure manually using *Maple*'s addrow, mulrow, and swaprow commands on the matrix A_B.

You use mulrow *to multiply a row by a scalar.*

- `mulrow(A_B,1,1/2);`

The matrix name comes first, then the number of the row to be multiplied, and then the multiplier. In this example, the first row is multiplied by 1/2.

You use addrow *to add a multiple of one row to another row.*

- `addrow(",1,2,-3);`

The first argument is the matrix (in this case, referenced by the ditto marks), the second argument is the number of the row to be multiplied, followed by the number of the row to which the multiple is to be added, followed by the multiplier.

You use swaprow *to interchange the order of two rows.*

- `swaprow(",2,3);`

Again, the first argument is the matrix, followed by the numbers of the rows to be interchanged.

Continue until you reach row echelon form.

- `mulrow(",2,3/2);`
- `R:=mulrow(",3,5/4);`

---

[1]The matrix A_B can be defined directly without defining A and B separately.
[2]You should never begin a name with the underscore character. *Maple* uses names of the form *_xxx* internally; the effect of assigning a value to such a name is unpredictable.

Apply back-substitution to the matrix

$$R = \begin{bmatrix} 1 & \dfrac{1}{2} & 2 & \dfrac{41}{8} \\[2ex] 0 & 1 & \dfrac{15}{2} & \dfrac{105}{8} \\[2ex] 0 & 0 & 1 & -\dfrac{1435}{96} \end{bmatrix}$$

to obtain the solution of the original system.

The value of x_3 is obvious.
- `x[3]:=-1435/96;`
This is a direct translation of the last row of the matrix R.

This solves for x_2.
- `x[2]:=105/8 - 15/2*x[3];`
This follows from the second row of R.

And this completes the solution.
- `x[1]:=41/8 - 1/2*x[2] - 2*x[3];`
This follows from the first row of R.

This verifies the solution for the first equation.
- `j:='j';`
- `sum(A[1,j]*x[j],j=1..3);`
You can verify the second and third equations in a similar fashion.

The variables x_1, x_2, x_3 retain their value throughout the remainder of the session, unless they are reassigned.

Recall the difference between x_1 and $'x_1'$.
- `x[1];`
- `'x[1]';`
In general, if `var` is a variable name, the value of `'var'` is the name "var" itself.

This has the effect of unassigning the variables x_1, x_2, and x_3.
- `x[1]:='x[1]';`
- `x[2]:='x[2]';`
- `x[3]:='x[3]';`
This assigns the variables their original unassigned values.

A typical row reduction of an $m \times n$ matrix requires approximately $m(m-1)/2$ applications of `addrow`, m applications of `mulrow`, and few—if any—applications of `swaprow`. Most of the work is done by `addrow`. You might wish to investigate the `pivot` command, which uses `addrow` to automatically zero the entries above and below a specified entry. Type `?pivot` for more information.

1.2.2 Automated Gaussian Elimination and Back-Substitution
[gaussjord, gausselim, rref, backsub]

In addition to the manual elementary row operations addrow, mulrow, and swaprow, *Maple* also offers automated procedures for Gaussian elimination. For example, the gausselim procedure can be used to take a matrix to row echelon form—although it does not make ones of the leading nonzero entries.

If necessary, re-enter the augmented matrix of the system that was solved in Section 1.2.1.

$$
\begin{aligned}
2x_1 + x_2 \quad + 4x_3 \quad &= \frac{41}{4} \\
3x_1 + \frac{3}{2}x_2 + \frac{34}{5}x_3 &= \frac{41}{12} \\
\frac{2}{3}x_2 + 5x_3 \quad &= \frac{35}{4}
\end{aligned}
$$

The matrix of the system was called A_B in Section 1.2.1.

- A_B:=matrix(
» [[2,1,4,41/4],
» [3,3/2,34/5,41/12],
» [0,2/3,5,35/4]]);

You can automate Gaussian elimination with the gausselim command.

- G:=gausselim(A_B);

Note that the result is not quite the same as that obtained in the previous section. In particular, the leading nonzero entries of the rows are not ones.

You can use the backsub command to automate the process of back-substitution.

Use backsub to automate back-substitution.

- X:=backsub(G);

The result is returned as a one-dimensional array $X = [x_1, x_2, x_3]$. The ith element of X is denoted X[i], so x_i = X[i], $i = 1 \ldots 3$. Note that the result agrees with that obtained in Section 1.2.1.

Maple provides other procedures for Gaussian elimination in addition to gausselim. Of particular importance is one called gaussjord or rref.

The gaussjord procedure reduces a matrix to reduced row echelon form.

- gaussjord(A_B);

The Gauss-Jordan procedure for solving linear systems is based on this reduction. By definition, in this case, the leading nonzero entries of the rows of the result are ones, and the entries above (and below) those ones are zeros.

Alternatively, you can use rref as a synonym for gaussjord.

- rref(A_B);

The command rref is an abbreviation for *reduced row echelon form*.

The reduced row echelon form is preferred by some over an arbitrary echelon form, at least in part because of its uniqueness. Many matrices that are in echelon form can be obtained from A_B by elementary row operations, but only one can be obtained that is in reduced row echelon form. It is also particularly easy to do back-substitution from reduced row echelon form. On the other hand, many numerical analysts argue that it is more efficient to do only the forward elimination before applying back-substitution. Of course, efficiency will also vary with the algorithms used.

EXERCISES 1.2 _____

1. Use `addrow`, `mulrow`, `swaprow`, and back-substitution to solve the systems in Exercises 1–4. Verify your solutions.

$$3x_2 - 4x_3 + \frac{5}{3}x_4 = \frac{23}{12}$$

$$2x_1 + 7x_2 + \frac{4}{3}x_3 + 3x_4 = \frac{41}{4}$$

$$\frac{1}{2}x_1 - 3x_2 + 2x_3 + \frac{13}{3}x_4 = \frac{41}{12}$$

$$\frac{7}{6}x_1 + \frac{7}{3}x_2 - \frac{14}{9}x_3 + 7x_4 = \frac{35}{4}$$

2. $3x_1 + 2x_2 - 3x_3 + 4x_4 = 5$
   $2x_1 + 7x_2 + 11x_3 - 3x_4 = 41$
   $2x_1 - 5x_2 + 3x_3 + 5x_4 = 12$
   $6x_1 + 3x_2 - 49x_3 + 2x_4 = 34$

3. $3x_1 + 2x_2 - 3x_3 + 4x_4 = 5$
   $2x_1 + 7x_2 + 11x_3 - 3x_4 = 41$

4. $2x_1 + 3x_2 + 3x_3 - 2x_4 = 3$
   $x_1 + 2x_2 + x_3 - x_4 = 1$
   $4x_1 + 7x_2 + 5x_3 - 4x_4 = 12$

5. Use `pivot`, `mulrow`, and back-substitution to solve the system of Exercise 2.

6. Use row reduction and back-substitution to solve the linear system with coefficient matrix C and constant matrix K, where $C = [c_{ij}]$ is the 3×5 matrix with $c_{ij} = (i + j)/j$ and $K = [k_{ij}]$ is the 3×1 matrix with $k_{ij} = 1$, $i = 1 \ldots 3$, $j = 1$. Verify the solution.

7. Repeat Exercise 6 for the following pairs of matrices.
   a. $C = [c_{ij}]$ is the 5×4 matrix with $c_{ij} = i/j$ and $K = [k_{ij}]$ is the 5×1 matrix with $k_{ij} = i$, $i = 1 \ldots 5$, $j = 1$.
   b. $C = [c_{ij}]$ is the 4×6 matrix with $c_{ij} = \max(i,j)$ and $K = [k_{ij}]$ is the 4×1 matrix with $k_{ij} = i!$, $i = 1 \ldots 4$, $j = 1$.

8. It is possible to specify a second argument with either `gausselim` or `gaussjord` that limits the columns from which the pivotal entries can be taken. For example, the command `gausselim(A, 2)` would stop the reduction process as soon as work on the first two columns was completed. The optional parameter can be used to find a linear system whose solutions are all the columns B for which the system with augmented matrix $[A,B]$ has a solution.

Execute the following code, and then describe the set of all columns B for which the linear system with coefficient matrix A and constant matrix B has a solution.

This defines the coefficient matrix A of the system in the session.

```
• A:=matrix(
» [[1,2,3,4,5,6,7],
»  [2,3,4,5,6,7,8],
»  [3,4,5,6,7,8,9],
»  [4,5,6,7,8,9,10],
»  [5,6,7,8,9,10,11]]);
```

The format of the input is a matter of personal preference; you can break the definition at any convenient points.

This generates a matrix of unknowns.

```
• B:=matrix(
[[b1],[b2],[b3],[b4],[b5]]);
```

Augment the matrix A by B.

```
• A_B:=augment(A,B);
```

Row-reduce the augmented matrix, limiting the pivots to the columns from A.

```
• G:=rref(A_B,7);
```

The system is consistent if and only if the first nonzero entry of every row is in the "A section" of the reduced matrix. Hence, for consistency, it is necessary that you have $G[3,8] = G[4,8] = G[5,8] = 0$.

9. Solve the linear system $\{G[3,8] = 0, G[4,8] = 0, G[5,8] = 0\}$ from Exercise 8 for $\{x_3, x_4, x_5\}$.

1.3 More on Matrices in *Maple*
[evalm]

Matrices are two-dimensional arrays and so their entries are addressed by two subscripts, as in

$$A = \begin{bmatrix} a_{11} & a_{12} \\ a_{21} & a_{22} \end{bmatrix}$$

where a_{ij} denotes the entry in the ith row and jth column. In *Maple*, the (i,j)-entry is denoted $A[i,j]$.

You can define matrices in several ways in *Maple*, using the `matrix` command. The variations and options are summarized in the `matrix` help page (type `?matrix` for further information). Three common forms are shown here; additional variations are explored in the exercises at the end of this section.

- `matrix(m,n,[...])`
- `matrix(m,n,[[...],...,[...]])`
- `matrix(m,n,f)`

In *Maple*, a sequence of objects enclosed in square brackets is a *list*. The first of the three common forms of the `matrix` command uses a simple list. The second form uses a list of lists; the inner lists are the individual rows of the matrix. The third form uses a "generating function." When the second form is used, the specification of the matrix dimensions (*m* and *n*) is optional.

If you are starting a new session, remember to reload the linalg *package.*

- `with(linalg);`

This defines the 4 × 3 matrix

$$\begin{bmatrix} 11 & 21 & 13 \\ 21 & 22 & 23 \\ 31 & 32 & 33 \\ 41 & 42 & 43 \end{bmatrix}$$

with a list of lists.

- `A:=matrix(`
- » `[[11,21,13],`
- » `[21,22,23],`
- » `[31,32,33],`
- » `[41,42,43]]);`

The argument is a list of lists. The inner lists are the rows of the matrix.

This defines the column matrix

$$K = \begin{bmatrix} 5 \\ 4 \\ 3 \\ 2 \\ 1 \end{bmatrix}$$

using a simple list.

- `K:=matrix(5,1,[5,4,3,2,1]);`

Maple breaks the rows as if the inner lists of the first form of the `matrix` command had been used.

The third form of the `matrix` command uses a generating function. It can be used with either built-in or user-defined functions. *Maple* will use the function specified to compute the entries and generate the matrix.

Here Maple's built-in maximum function is used.

- `M:=matrix(5,5,max);`

Note that the (i,j)-entry, $M[i,j]$, is the maximum of the subscripts i and j.

Recall that *Maple* supports two styles of definition for user-defined functions: the *arrow* style and the `proc` style. The first is named for the notation it uses. The second is a contraction of the word *procedure*. The arrow style is useful for functions that apply the same rule to all elements in their domain. More complicated functions require the `proc` style. Both styles are demonstrated in the following.

Here, the function $g(i,j) = i^2 - j$ is defined in the arrow style and used to generate an 8×9 matrix with (i,j)-entry $i^2 - j$.

- `g:=(i,j)->i^2-j;`

- `B:=matrix(8,9,g);`

Note that the (i,j)-entry of B is $g(i,j) = i^2 - j$.

Here, the function

$$f(i, j) = \begin{cases} i^j & \text{if } i < j \\ j^i & \text{otherwise} \end{cases}$$

is defined and used to generate a 24×12 matrix in which the (i,j)-entry is $f(i,j)$.

- `f:=proc(i,j)`
- » `if i<j then i^j`
- » `  else j^i fi`
- » `end;`

- `M:=matrix(24,12,f);`

When applicable, the use of a generating function in this manner is extremely convenient, especially in the definition of large matrices.

It is also possible to define a matrix using an unnamed function by giving the definition of the generating function as the third argument.

Here, a simple arrow definition is given as the third argument to the `matrix` *command.*

- `N:=matrix(7,7,(i,j)->i-j^2);`

Here, the 7×7 matrix ID = $[d_{ij}]$ defined by

$$d_{ij} = \begin{cases} 1 & \text{if } i = j \\ 0 & \text{otherwise} \end{cases}$$

is defined using a `proc` *definition. (The generating function is known as the Kronecker delta function.)*

- `ID:=matrix(7,7,`
- » `proc(i,j) if i=j then 1 else 0 fi end);`

Note that there is no semicolon immediately after the end statement of the definition of the function.

Reviewing and Editing Matrix Definitions

At some point, you will almost certainly want to review, and possibly edit, the entries of a matrix you have already defined.

Maple does not respond to a matrix name by displaying the contents of the matrix.

- A;

The matrix *A* was defined earlier in the session.

You use the evalm *command to tell Maple to display the standard rectangular form of an array.*

- evalm(A);

You might think of evalm as meaning "evaluate as a matrix."

You can access the (i,j)-entry of A as A[i,j].

- A[1,2];

This is sometimes called "computer subscript notation."

To modify an entry, you simply reassign it. Here, the (1, 2)-entry of A is changed to 12.

- A[1,2]:=12;

You may wish to use evalm to see the full matrix with the entry changed.

EXERCISES 1.3 _____

1. Define the following matrices in your *Maple* session.
   a. The 5×5 matrix $M = [m_{ij}]$ with

   $$m_{ij} = \begin{cases} 1 & \text{if } i \geq j \\ 2 & \text{otherwise} \end{cases}$$

   (*Maple* uses >= for $\geq$.)
   b. The 5×5 matrix $N = [n_{ij}]$ with

   $$n_{ij} = \begin{cases} 0 & \text{if } i = j \\ 1 & \text{otherwise} \end{cases}$$

   c. The 1×5 matrix $R = [1,5,2,3,4]$.
   d. The 5×1 matrix $C = [c_{ij}]$ defined by $c_{ij} = 1/i$.
2. Define the 10×10 matrix $N = [n_{ij}]$ in your *Maple* session, where $n_{ij} = i^2 + 3i - j^3 + 2j - 1$.
3. The matrix R of Exercise 1c is a row. Why does *Maple* return an error message in response to the statement R[1]?
4. In standard mathematical notation, the symbol 3 is used to denote both the number 3 and the constant functions $f(x) = 3$, $f(x,y) = 3$, etc. Given this, how would you expect *Maple* to respond to the commands M:=matrix(5,5,3); and N:=matrix(5,5,k);? Verify your answers.

5. Assume $L[1]$: = [1,2,3,4], $L[2]$: = [2,3,4,5], $L[3]$: = [3,4,5,6] and LL: = [$L[1],L[2],L[3]$].
   a. Explain *Maple*'s response to the command `matrix(LL);`.
   b. Explain *Maple*'s response to the command
      `matrix(4,1,L[1]);`.
6. What do you think will happen if you use a colon at the end of a *Maple* command, instead of a semicolon? For comparative purposes, issue the commands `a:=3:` and `b:=";`. (The colon is *Maple*'s silent terminator; you may find that you prefer to use it to suppress intermediate output that is not of interest—especially if the output is long.)

1.4 Matrix Arithmetic
```
[ &*, *, +, -, ^, /, &*(), alias,
inverse, multiply, add ]
```

Maple uses the same notation for most arithmetic operations with matrices that it uses with numbers. One exception is that the usual multiplication symbol (*) is reserved for scalar multiplication; the compound symbol ampersand-star (&*) is used for matrix multiplication. Table 1.1 summarizes *Maple*'s arithmetic operators.

You can use `evalm` to get the fully evaluated, standard form of any matrix expression involving the functions in Table 1.1. However, you *need* only call `evalm` when you want the result in standard rectangular form—intermediate calculations can often be done without viewing the results in standard form.

Table 1.1

Operation	Standard notation	*Maple* notation[3]
Addition	$A + B$	A + B
Subraction	$A - B$	A - B
Scalar multiplication	$k A$	k*A
	$\frac{1}{k} A$	A/k
Matrix multiplication	AB	A &* B
Powers	A^n	A^n
Inverse	A^{-1}	A^(-1)
		1/A

[3]A space is required after `&*` if it is followed by the ditto symbol (").

- with(linalg):

From this point on, we will use the silent terminator with the with statement (see Exercise 6 in Section 1.3).

Enter the matrices A and B to use as examples.

The matrices A and B will be used in the sequel.

- A:=matrix(3,3,min);
- B:=matrix(3,5,max);

You build an arithmetic matrix expression as you would a numerical arithmetic expression, except that you use &* for matrix products.

- C:=A &* B + B;
- D:=A^2 &* B - B;
- F:=1/2 * 1/A &*(C + D);

Note the simplification that takes place before evalm is applied.

Use evalm to get the evaluated result in standard matrix form.

- evalm(");

You might find it convenient to define a macro to do this (for more information, see Section 0.3.19).

If you wish to view the (perhaps simplified) definition of the expression F rather than the value of the expression, you can use the print command.

- print(F);

If print is applied to a matrix name, the matrix will be printed in standard rectangular form; however, more complicated expressions such as F are not fully evaluated.

Note that print does not change the reference of the ditto symbol (").

- ";

This property makes print nearly unique among *Maple* commands—the help command shares this property.

It is also possible to "wrap" expressions with evalm, using standard function notation.

- evalm(A &* B + B);

If an expression will not be reused, there is no need to name it.

Applying evalm only when the standard form is required saves both time and screen space. However, you will find your own style as you proceed—think of evalm as a button to push whenever you want to see the evaluated form of your matrix calculation.

Following standard convention, *Maple* will sometimes use 0 to denote a zero matrix.

This gives the single symbol 0 a number of meanings.

- A - A;

In this case, application of evalm gives no additional information.

You can use 0 in this way as a generic zero matrix as well.

- `0 + A;`
- `0 &* A;`
- `evalm(");`

Note that the simplification is not automatic with `&*`.

In its initial configuration, *Maple* uses the unappealing compound symbol `&*()` for a generic identity matrix. However, *Maple*'s developers did not expect that you would want to leave it that way—you can use the `alias` command to reset it to the symbol of your choice. The most natural choice, *I*, is initially used to denote $\sqrt{-1}$, but aliasing *I* to `&*()` will simply cause *Maple* to respond $(-1)^{1/2}$ when it would otherwise have used the symbol *I*.

If you prefer to leave *I* aliased to $\sqrt{-1}$, some of the alias choices of other users for `&*()` are "Id," "II," "Eye," and "eye." We will use Id.

If you do not "alias" it, you may be surprised to find that Maple thinks the name of the product of a matrix and its inverse is `&*()`.

- `evalm(1/A &* A);`

Another choice of symbols may seem more natural.

You can reconfigure your session so that Maple will use another name in place of `&*()`.

- `alias(Id=&*());`

The `alias` command can be used to set an abbreviation or new name for virtually any expression. Note that *Maple* responds with a list of all current aliases.

Now, both you and Maple can use the new name in place of the old.

- `evalm((1/A)&* Id &* A);`

That looks a bit better.

You should note that Maple may assume you will not take the inverse of a singular matrix.

- `evalm(1/B &* B);`

The answer is clearly incorrect; the matrix *B* is not even square. In this case, *Maple* "simplifies" the expression without attempting to compute the inverse.

You can use the matrix Id to generate "hard-coded" identity matrices if you wish.

This assigns the name I3 to the 3 × 3 identity matrix.

- `I3:= evalm(matrix(3,3,0)+Id);`

Names such as *I3* are often used as a convenient alternative form of subscripting. Recall that `backsub` uses this form of subscripting for parameters.

Under addition and subtraction, *Maple* will also let you use a scalar *k* as an abbreviation for the scalar matrix *kI*. This is helpful in evaluating matrix polynomials (matrix expressions of the form $\sum_{i=0}^{k} a_i A^i$).

You can use a scalar k as shorthand for the scalar matrix kI for addition and subtraction.

- `evalm(A + 3);`

Note that this is equivalent to `evalm(A + 3*Id)`.

If you prefer, you can use *Maple*'s inverse command instead of `evalm(1/M)` to get the inverse of a matrix.[4]

The inverse *command does not require the use of* evalm.

- `inverse(A);`

You may wish to compare the result with that produced by `evalm(1/A)`.

The inverse *command returns an error message if you attempt to invert a singular matrix.*

- `evalm(inverse(B) &* B);`

The expression `evalm(1/B &* B)` is evaluated symbolically without checking if B is invertible; this is not the case with `evalm(inverse(B) &* B)`.

Note that definitions made in a *Maple* session are valid for that session only. Definitions can be saved to disk and loaded into a new session, but otherwise they will be unknown to *Maple* after the close of the session in which they are defined.

1.4.1   A Few Pitfalls to Avoid

In evaluating an expression such as 1/B &* B, *Maple just "simplifies" the expression.*

- `evalm(1/B &* B);`

Note that the matrix B is not invertible—it is not even square.

Matrix expressions of the form B &* (1/A) *must be parenthesized.*

- `B &* 1/A;`

The numerator is an illegal expression; if you apply `evalm`, you will get an error message. Try it!

In an expression of the form A &* ", *the* &* *and the* " *must be separated by a space.*

- `B;`
- `evalm(A &*");`

Maple interprets `&*"` as an undefined operation.

Note that matrix expressions of the form *B/A* are illegal in *Maple* whether or not *A* is invertible.

1.4.2   Legal Names

You are free to use as many characters in a name as you choose. For example, you could use "SumOfAandB" for the sum of two matrices *A* and *B*.

---

[4]Maple also has `multiply` and `add` commands that can be used in place of `evalm(A &* B)` and `evalm(A+B)`. If you want more information on these commands, use `?mulitply` and `?add`.

However, *Maple* will not gracefully accept names that contain spaces or names that begin with numbers (though it can be tricked into doing so by enclosing the name in back quotes). There are also certain reserved characters that should not or cannot be used. You will have no problem if you stick to standard names of the sort used in this text. On the other hand, if you try to use characters such as %, @, and so forth, *Maple* will respond with "syntax error," which is just the system's way of saying you have violated *Maple*'s rules and does no harm to the system. You should also avoid names that begin with the underscore character (_): *Maple* uses names of the form *_name* as global variables. If you assign a value to a global variable, commands and functions using that variable internally will not function correctly. (Variables of the form _C1, _C2, and so on are an exception to this rule: *Maple* checks to see if a variable with a name of the form _Cn is assigned before using it.)

The most common convention for naming matrices is to use single uppercase letters, such as *A, B, C,* and so on. Or, particularly if a family of related matrices is defined, subscripts are commonly used. You may choose a notation such as *A*1, *A*2, and so forth. However, it is legal, and often desirable, to use names such as *A*[1], *A*[2], and so on. The effect is to implicitly create a *table* in your session. A table is rather like an array, but it offers more flexibility in the choice of indices—for example, you can name a matrix *A*[red].

Here are two points to note regarding the use of tables:

- You cannot use a name of the form *A*[*i*] if *A* has been defined as a matrix; in this case, use of the notation *A*[1] results in an error message.
- The table created by assigning values to *A*[1], *A*[2], and so on, is named *A*. You can view the table by using the print command. If you assign a value to *A*, you will lose the definitions of *A*[1], *A*[2], and so forth.

First, unassign A.

- `A:='A';`

A was assigned a matrix value earlier.

This defines a table named A with two matrix entries.

- `A[1]:=matrix(3,3,max);`
- `A[2]:=matrix(3,3,min);`

You can use the print *command to see the table.*

- `print(A);`

You can use evalm *to see either of the matrices in the table, as usual.*

- `evalm(A[1]);`

This assigns A the 3×3 *zero matrix as its value.*

- `A:=matrix(3,3,0);`

The table was destroyed in the process and the definitions of A[1] and A[2] are lost.

- `evalm(A[1]);`

A is now a matrix. *Maple* expects two subscripts for an entry address of *A*.

You cannot now recreate A as a table without first unassigning the name A.

- `A[1]:=matrix(3,3,max);`

A is a matrix, so *A*[1] has no meaning. This is why *A* was unassigned at the beginning of this sequence of calculations.

This unassigns the variable A and frees it for other use.

- `A:='A';`

Recall that the quoted variable regains its original value—in this case, the letter *A*. Notice that we are now back at the beginning of the command sequence.

You can now define A[1] if you wish.

- `A[1]:=matrix(3,3,max);`

If you get an error message when you attempt such a definition, chances are that unassigning *A* will cure the problem—if you don't need the definition any longer.

1.4.3   Random Matrices
[randmatrix, sparse]

If you are testing a hypothesis and want to have some random examples, you can use *Maple*'s `randmatrix` command to generate random integer matrices.

This generates a "random" 5 × 5 integer matrix.

- `randmatrix(5,5);`

You could use `randmatrix` to generate matrices to test the probability that *AB = BA*, for example.

If you want a matrix with a lot of zeros, you can use the `sparse` *option.*

- `randmatrix(10,10,sparse);`

You might want to test several matrices to get an idea of the probability that a square matrix is invertible.

1.4.4   Symbolic Matrices
[rand]

You can also do arithmetic with matrices having either undefined entries or entries that are undefined variables; we will call these "symbolic matrices." In many cases, symbolic matrices can be used to prove results in low dimensions.

This defines a matrix with undefined entries.

- `M:=matrix(2,2);`

Note *Maple*'s response.

Maple's response to the evalm *command is more as expected.*

- `evalm(M);`

`M[i,j]` can be thought of as undefined or defined to be itself.

Here Maple calculates the familiar formula for the inverse of an invertible 2 × 2 matrix.

- `evalm(1/M);`

This is, in effect, a proof of the standard formula for the inverse of a 2 × 2 matrix.

This defines a 2 × 2 matrix with undefined variables as entries.

- `S:=matrix(2,2,[a,b,c,d]);`

If any of the symbols *a, b, c,* and *d* had an assigned value, they would be replaced by the value.

Symbolic matrices can be used in all the same ways as numerical matrices.

- `evalm(Id &* S);`

The following uses symbolic matrices to give a computational proof of the associative law *A*(*BC*) = (*AB*)*C* for 3 × 3 matrices. The same technique can be used to establish other properties for matrices of a fixed size.

Define three 3 × 3 matrices for the proof.

- `A:=matrix(3,3);`
- `B:=matrix(3,3);`
- `C:=matrix(3,3);`

Calculate the two sides of the equation.

- `LHS:=evalm(A &* (B &* C)):`
- `RHS:=evalm((A &* B)&* C):`

The descriptions of the matrices are quite long and superfluous, so the silent terminator (:) can be used.

This picks out the (2,3)-entries for comparison. Perhaps this will inspire an idea.

- `LHS[2,3];`
- `RHS[2,3];`

The terms are large, but they are small enough to compare. *Maple* can determine easily if the two are the same by checking to see if their difference is 0.

This shows that the (2,3)-entries of LHS and RHS are the same.

- `LHS[2,3]-RHS[2,3];`

Repeating this operation for the other eight positions would constitute a proof.

Matrix subtraction seems to be the answer.

- `evalm(LHS-RHS);`

The result establishes the equality *LHS = RHS*.

Note that *Maple* does not always simplify expressions automatically. To force a simplification of the entries of a matrix *M*, use the *Maple* command `map(simplify,M)`. A similar syntax is used to apply any function to the entries of a matrix.

EXERCISES 1.4 _____

1. Let $A = [a_{ij}]$ be the 5×5 matrix defined by the equation $a_{ij} = 1/(i + j - 1)$. Let $B = [b_{ij}]$ be the 5×6 matrix defined by the equation $b_{ij} = i + j - 1$. Let $C = [c_{ij}]$ be the 5×6 matrix defined by the equation $b_{ij} = 1/(j + 1)$. Determine which of the following expressions are defined, and evaluate those that are.

    a. AB b. $A(B + C)$ c. $AB + AC$
    d. $A(B - C)$ e. $AB - AC$ f. $A(BC)$
    g. $(AB)C$ h. A^5 i. $A^{-1}A^6$
    j. $A + 3\,\text{Id}$ k. $\text{Id}\,A$ l. $A^3 - 3A + \text{Id}$

2. Let $M = [m_{ij}]$ be the 2×2 matrix defined by $m_{ij} = \max(i,j)$. Let $N = [n_{ij}]$ be the 2×2 matrix defined by $n_{ij} = \min(i,j)$. Show that $MN \neq NM$. Repeat the exercise for the $n \times n$ analogs of M and N, $n = 3,10,11$.

3. Let $A = [a_{ij}]$ be the 3×3 matrix defined by the equation $a_{ij} = i^2 - j^2$. Define $p = x^3 + 98x$. Use the `subs` command to replace x by A in the expression. Evaluate the expression to get $p(A)$. Note that the answer implies that $A(A^2 + 98I) = 0$, hence A is not invertible; explain why. What happens in this case if you try to compute the inverse in *Maple*, using either the `inverse` command or $1/A$?

4. Let $A = [a_{ij}]$ be the 5×5 matrix defined by the equation $a_{ij} = \max(i,j)$. Let p be the polynomial generated by the *Maple* command `det(x*Id - A)`. Use the `subs` command to substitute A for x in p and show that the resulting matrix polynomial evaluates to 0. Use this to find the inverse of A. (You will investigate the polynomial p more later.)

5. Randomly generate ten square matrices and try to invert them. Based on your calculations, what do you estimate the probability to be that an arbitrary square, real matrix is invertible?

6. Use 3×3 matrices with unassigned entries to give a computational proof of the 3×3 case of the distributive law

    $$(A + B)\,C = AC + BC$$

7. What is the difference, if any, in *Maple* between $1/A$ `&*` B and $1/($ A `&*` $B)$?

8. Let M be the symbolic matrix obtained from the definition `M:=matrix(10,10)`. Verify that *Maple* responds to the command `evalm(1/(1/M))` with the matrix M. Why is this not a computational proof in the same sense that Exercise 6 is?

9. Use symbolic matrices to give a computational proof for 5×5 matrices that $(kI)A = kA = A(kI)$, for all scalars k.

Exercises 10, 11, and 12 use *Maple*'s `rand` command.

10. You can use *Maple*'s `rand` command to generate random numbers or to generate a function that will generate random numbers in a given range: the command `rand()` will generate a random 24-digit integer;

the command `rand(m..n)` will generate a function that will generate random integers in the range $m, \ldots, n$ (where m and n are integers with $m < n$).

The `rand` *command will generate random integers.*

- `rand();`

  427419669081

You can also use the `rand` *command to create a function that will generate random integers in a specified range.*

- `Myrand:=rand(-100..-1);`

```
proc( )
local t;
    _seed := irem(427419669081*_seed,999999999989);
    t := _seed;
    irem(t,100)-100
end
```

Use the `Myrand` command to generate a 5×5 matrix with quasi-random rational entries a/b with both a and b between -100 and 100.

11. A matrix $A = [a_{ij}]$ with the property that $a_{ij} = 0$ whenever $i > j$ is said to be upper-triangular.

     a. Define a function $f(i,j)$ that will return random integer entries if $i \leq j$ and 0 otherwise. (See Exercise 10.)

     b. Use the function f to generate two random upper-triangular 6×6 matrices M and N.

     c. Verify that the product MN is upper-triangular.

12. A matrix $A = [a_{ij}]$ with the property that $a_{ij} = 0$ whenever $i \geq j$ is said to be *strictly* upper-triangular.

     a. Define a function $g(i,j)$ that will return random integer entries if $i < j$ and 0 if $i \geq j$. (See Exercise 10.)

     b. Use the function g to generate a 5×5 matrix A.

     c. Compute A^5.

     d. Repeat parts b and c for a variety of matrices and exponents. Can you form a conjecture regarding the nth power of a strictly upper-triangular matrix?

13. A matrix M satisfying $M^n = 0$ and $M^{n-1} \neq 0$ is said to be nilpotent of *index n.* Based on experimentation, what would you conjecture about the index of nilpotency of a strictly upper-triangular $n \times n$ matrix?

14. The generating function for a matrix can place variables as well as numbers in the matrix. One easy way to do this is to use *Maple*'s concatenation operator (.).

This function will generate a matrix that is partially symbolic and partially numeric.

```
 •  ut:=proc(i,j)
 »      if i<j then x.i.j
 »      else 0
 »    fi
 »  end;
```

Use ut *to generate a* 5 × 5 *matrix.*	• T:=matrix(5,5,ut); Note that *T* is strictly upper-triangular.

        a.   Use the matrix *T* to give a computational proof that the fifth power of a 5 × 5 strictly upper-triangular matrix is 0.

        b.   What can you say about T^2, T^3, T^4?

  15. Show that every strictly upper-triangular $n \times n$ matrix *T* is nilpotent of index ≤ n (in other words, satisfies $T^n = 0$).

1.5 **det** and Other Built-in Matrix Functions
[det, adjoint, transpose, submatrix, rank]

The standard, basic matrix commands and functions—together with a number of more specialized ones— are built into *Maple*'s linalg package.

If you have not already done so.	• with(linalg); • alias(Id=&*());
Define the matrix A for use as an example.	• A:=matrix(5,5,min);
You can compute the determinant of a matrix.	• det(A);
You can compute the adjoint of a matrix—not a favorite pastime for many when computing by hand.	• Adj:=adjoint(A); The calculation of the adjoint of a 5 × 5 matrix requires the calculation of the determinants of twenty-five 4 × 4 matrices.
You can compute the transpose of a matrix.	• transpose(A); You may wish to alias transpose to a shorter name—perhaps trans or T.
You can extract submatrices —this gives the upper-left-hand corner of A.	• submatrix(A,1..4,1..4); See the help page on submatrix for all the forms of this command.
You can compute the rank of a matrix.	• rank(A); An $n \times n$ matrix is invertible if and only if it has rank n.

You can use the det command to investigate the properties of the determinant function. These are explored in the following exercises.

EXERCISES 1.5 _____

1. Verify the identity $A \text{ adj}(A) = \text{adj}(A) A = \det(A) I$ for a randomly generated 5×5 matrix.

2. Verify the identity $\text{adj}(A)^T = \text{adj}(A^T)$ for a randomly generated 4×4 matrix.

3. For a randomly generated 8×8 matrix A, verify that the matrix B obtained by interchanging the first two rows of A satisfies $\det(B) = -\det(A)$.

4. For a randomly generated 6×6 matrix A, verify that any matrix obtained by adding a multiple of the first row to the second has the same determinant.

5. For a randomly generated 7×7 matrix A, verify that $\det(A) = \det(A^T)$.

6. Let C_{ij} denote the (i,j)-cofactor of A. (Recall that the (i,j)-cofactor is given by $(-1)^{i+j}\det(M_{ij})$, where M_{ij} is the submatrix of A obtained by deleting the ith row and jth column.) Verify the Lagrange identities

   a. $\det(A) = \displaystyle\sum_{j=1}^{n} a_{ij}C_{ij}, i = 1..n$

   b. $\det(A) = \displaystyle\sum_{i=1}^{n} a_{ij}C_{ij}, j = 1..n$

   c. $\displaystyle\sum_{j=1}^{n} a_{rj}C_{sj} = \sum_{j=1}^{n} a_{ir}C_{is} = 0 \text{ if } r \neq s$

   for a randomly generated 4×4 matrix A. (Hint: See Exercise 1.)

7. Use mathematical induction to verify the identities $\text{adj}(A)^T = \text{adj}(A^T)$ and $\det(A) = \det(A^T)$ for all square matrices.

In Exercises 8–12, use a matrix with undefined entries to prove each statement.

8. A 4×4 matrix and its transpose have the same determinant.

9. For all 4×4 matrices A, $\text{adj}(A)^T = \text{adj}(A^T)$ and $\det(A) = \det(A^T)$.

10. Interchanging the first two rows of a 4×4 matrix changes the sign of the determinant.

11. Adding a multiple of the first row to the second row of a 4×4 matrix does not affect the determinant.

12. Multiplying the first row of a 4×4 matrix by a scalar k changes the determinant by a multiple of k.

1.6 Applications

Curve Fitting and Interpolation
[vandermonde, subs]

It is well known that two points determine a line. We also know that the equation of a nonvertical line has the form $y = a_0 + a_1x$. Hence, two points

(x_1,y_1) and (x_2,y_2), with $x_1 \neq x_2$), determine a linear equation $y = a_0 + a_1x$ such that

$$\begin{cases} y_1 = a_0 + a_1x_1 \\ y_2 = a_0 + a_1x_2 \end{cases}$$

This system is easily solved for a_0 and a_1 using row reduction and back-substitution.

In general, $n + 1$ points (x_1,y_1), (x_2,y_2), ..., (x_{n+1},y_{n+1}) (with $x_i \neq x_j$ whenever $i \neq j$) determine a polynomial equation of the form $y = a_0 + a_1x + \cdots + a_nx^n$ that satisfies

$$\begin{cases} y_1 = a_0 + a_1x_1 + \cdots + a_nx_1{}^n \\ y_2 = a_0 + a_1x_2 + \cdots + a_nx_2{}^n \\ \qquad\qquad . \\ \qquad\qquad . \\ \qquad\qquad . \\ y_{n+1} = a_0 + a_1x_{n+1} + \cdots + a_nx_{n+1}{}^n \end{cases}$$

Again, this system is easily solved for the unknowns a_0, a_1, ..., a_n using row reduction and back-substitution.

For example, assume you know that the graph of a polynomial $p(x)$ of degree 5 or less passes through the six points (1,2), (2,3), (3,6), (4,7), (5,9), and (6,11), and you want to know the value of $p(x)$ at $x = 30$.

Make a list X of the x values.

• X:=[1,2,3,4,5,6];
The ith entry of X is denoted $X[i]$; hence $X[i] = x_i$.

Enter the matrix $M = [x_i^{j-1}]$. (We use the convention here that $x_i^0 = 1$.)[5]

• M:=matrix(6,6,(i,j)->X[i]^(j-1));
A matrix of this form is called a Vandermonde matrix; the function definition would require correction if one of the x_i were 0.

Define the column Y of y values.

• Y:=matrix(6,1,
» [2,3,6,7,9,13]);
Form the augmented matrix $[M,Y]$ to find the coefficients.

Solve for the coefficients a_i.

• M_Y:=augment(M,Y);
• gausselim(M_Y);
• a:=backsub(");
Now a is a one-dimensional array and $a_i = a[i]$.

[5]This matrix can also be obtained using *Maple*'s built-in vandermonde command. Use ?vandermonde for more information.

Define the polynomial p
with coefficients a_i.

- `p:=a[1]+a[2]*x+a[3]*x^2+a[4]*x^3+`
» `a[5]*x^4+a[6]*x^5;`

You might prefer to use the `sum` command to do this.

You can use `subs` *to find*
the value of p for any value
of x.

- `subs(x=30,p);`

In functional notation, this is $p(30)$.

If you wish, you can define p so that it is a polynomial function rather than a polynomial expression.

The `sum` *command provides*
a compact form of the
definition.

- `i:='i';`
- `p:=x->sum(a[i+1]*x^i,i=0..5);`

The indices for **a** run from 1 to 6.

You can now easily find the
value of p for any value of x.

- `p(35);`
- `p(50);`

This style follows standard mathematical notation more closely.

If you wish, you can `plot`
the function over an interval
of interest.

- `plot(p(x),x=22..35);`

It is also possible to specify the range of y values to be plotted. See the help page on `plot` for other alternatives.

Problems on Curve Fitting and Interpolation

1. Find the polynomial $p(x)$, of degree at most 8, having a graph that passes through the nine points $(-8,12)$, $(-6,23)$, $(-4,16)$, $(-2,23)$, $(1,0)$, $(2,23)$, $(4,16)$, $(6,23)$, and $(8,12)$. Plot its graph and find $p(7)$.
2. Find the polynomial $p(x)$, of degree at most 3, having a graph that passes through the four points $(-4,112)$, $(11,-128)$, $(2,70)$, and $(5,-140)$. Plot its graph and find $p(10)$.
3. Assume that in the years 1971 through 1990, water samples were tested in a midwestern U.S. community to determine their content of alphagen. The contents, in parts per million, are given by the following table.

Alphagen: 1971–1988

1971	1972	1973	1974	1975	1976
85	55	37	35	45	50

1977	1978	1979	1980	1981	1982
59	56	49	53	57	59

1983	1984	1985	1986	1987	1988
55	51	44	54	61	63

Environmentalists are concerned about the future concentration of alphagen. It is hypothesized that the alphagen content is a polynomial function of time, of degree 17. Based on this table, what do you expect the contents of alphagen to be in the year 1995? (Assume that the answer is given by the polynomial determined by the data points for the years 1971–1988.) Plot the graph of the function. Do the environmentalists have cause for concern?

Leontief Economic Model
[map]

The following problem is an introduction to the mathematical modeling of Wassily Leontief, who was awarded the Nobel prize in economics in 1973 for his work in mathematical models.

Assume a conglomerate consists of four industries—M_1 = coal, M_2 = energy, M_3 = steel, and M_4 = transportation and heavy equipment (bulldozers, cranes, and so on). Assume each of the industries buys all that it needs from the conglomerate and that all of its needs can be met from within the conglomerate. Let p_i be the total value, in millions of dollars, of the production of M_i. Let c_{ij} be the dollar value of M_i required to produce one dollar's worth of M_j. Let d_i be the value, in millions of dollars, of M_i consumed outside of the conglomerate over some convenient period of time. Assume that the c_{ij} and d_i are given by the following table.

	M_1	M_2	M_3	M_4		D
M_1 (coal)	.00	.42	.75	.00	d_1	12
M_2 (steel)	.01	.02	.01	.55	d_2	14
M_3 (energy)	.11	.40	.02	.27	d_3	38
M_4 (trans. & heavy equip.)	.21	.12	.05	.05	d_4	55

The problem is to determine the unknowns p_i so that all the product is used in exactly the same quantity in which it is produced. This leads to the following system of equations.

$$\begin{cases} c_{11}p_1 + c_{12}p_2 + c_{13}p_3 + c_{14}p_4 + d_1 = p_1 \\ c_{21}p_1 + c_{22}p_2 + c_{23}p_3 + c_{24}p_4 + d_2 = p_2 \\ c_{31}p_1 + c_{32}p_2 + c_{33}p_3 + c_{34}p_4 + d_3 = p_3 \\ c_{41}p_1 + c_{42}p_2 + c_{43}p_3 + c_{44}p_4 + d_4 = p_4 \end{cases}$$

The matrix $[c_{ij}]$ is called the *consumption matrix*. The matrix

$$P = \begin{bmatrix} p_1 \\ p_2 \\ p_3 \\ p_4 \end{bmatrix}$$

is called the *output matrix*. The matrix

$$D = \begin{bmatrix} 12 \\ 14 \\ 38 \\ 55 \end{bmatrix}$$

is called the *demand matrix*. Rearranging the terms produces the equivalent system

$$\begin{cases} (1 - c_{11})p_1 - & c_{12}p_2 - & c_{13}p_3 - & c_{14}p_4 = d_1 \\ -\ c_{21}p_1 + (1 - c_{22})p_2 - & c_{23}p_3 - & c_{24}p_4 = d_2 \\ -\ c_{31}p_1 - & c_{32}p_2 + (1 - c_{33}p_3) - & c_{34}p_4 = d_3 \\ -\ c_{41}p_1 - & c_{42}p_2 - & c_{43}p_3 + (1 - c_{44}p_4) = d_4 \end{cases}$$

The solution proceeds as follows. (The method used for generating the coefficient matrix of the system will also work well for larger problems; decimals are avoided to prevent cumulative rounding errors.)

This defines the consumption matrix C of the economy.

```
• C:=matrix(4,4,
» [0,42/100,75/100,0,
» 1/100,2/100,1/100,55/100,
» 11/100,40/100,2/100,27/100,
» 21/100,12/100,5/100,5/100]);
```

This defines a generating function for the coefficient matrix of the linear system to be solved.

```
• f:=proc(i,j)
»   if i=j then 1-C[i,j]
»     else -C[i,j]
»   fi
» end;
```

Use f to generate the coefficient matrix of the system.

```
• K:=matrix(4,4,f);
```

Define the demand matrix of the system.

```
• D:=matrix(4,1,[12,14,38,55]);
```

Create the augmented matrix of the system.

```
• augment(K,D);
```

Use Gaussian elimination to reduce the matrix to row echelon form.	• `gausselim(")`;
Following back-substitution, the value of p_i is now $p[i]$.	• `p:=backsub(")`;
If desired, you can convert the result to a matrix.	• `P:=matrix(4,1,(i,j)->p[i])`;
You can now convert to floating-point form without concern for cumulative rounding errors.	• `map(evalf,P)`;

The `evalf` function is used to convert fractions to decimals. The `map` command is used to cause `evalf` to work on the entries of the matrix.

Problems on the Leontief Model

1. Assume the economy of the country Elpmis consists of four distinct commodities M_1 = food, M_2 = shelter, M_3 = transportation, and M_4 = clothing—and that the consumption and demand matrices of the economy are given by

$$C = \frac{1}{100} \begin{bmatrix} 55 & 45 & 53 & 34 \\ 5 & 2 & 1 & 1 \\ 10 & 11 & 8 & 9 \\ 20 & 35 & 29 & 50 \end{bmatrix}, \quad D = \begin{bmatrix} 8/10 \\ 1 \\ 3/10 \\ 6/10 \end{bmatrix}$$

Find the output matrix in both exact and decimal forms.

2. The economy of Orcam consists of ten industries, $M_1, M_2, ..., M_{10}$. The consumption matrix is given by the generating function

```
F := (i,j)-> min(i+j mod 20,10)/100
```

and the demand matrix is given by the generating function

```
d:=(i,j)->abs(20-i^2)
```

Find the output matrix in both exact and decimal forms.

Incidence Matrices

An $n \times n$ matrix M consisting entirely of zeros and ones is called an *incidence matrix*. Incidence matrices arise naturally in connection-type problems; for example, in transportation problems where a one in the (i,j)-entry signifies a connection from the ith to the jth location, and a zero in the (i,j)-entry indicates the lack of a connection from the ith to the jth location.

Consider an airline that serves ten states S_1, S_2, ..., S_{10}. Assume the following array contains a one in the ith row and jth column if there is a direct flight from S_i to S_j, and a zero otherwise.

	S_1	S_2	S_3	S_4	S_5	S_6	S_7	S_8	S_9	S_{10}
S_1	0	1	0	0	0	0	0	0	0	1
S_2	0	0	1	0	0	0	0	0	0	0
S_3	1	0	0	0	0	0	0	0	0	0
S_4	0	0	0	0	1	0	0	0	0	1
S_5	0	0	0	0	0	1	0	0	0	0
S_6	0	0	0	1	0	0	0	0	0	0
S_7	0	0	0	0	0	0	0	1	0	1
S_8	0	0	0	0	0	0	0	0	1	1
S_9	0	0	0	0	0	0	1	0	0	0
S_{10}	1	0	0	1	0	0	1	0	0	0

One of the easiest ways to set up such a matrix is to set up the 10×10 zero matrix and then edit it. The editing can be automated as follows.

This defines a 10×10 zero matrix.

- `M:=matrix(10,10,0);`

Here, 0 acts as the zero function.

This sets up a list of the nonzero entries.

- `LL:=`
- » `[[1,2],[1,10],[2,3],[3,1],`
- » `[4,5],[4,10],[5,6],[6,4],`
- » `[7,8],[7,10],[8,9],[8,10],`
- » `[9,7],[10,1],[10,4],[10,7]];`

This changes the entries of A in the positions listed in LL to ones.

- `for L in LL`
- » `do`
- » `M[L[1],L[2]]:=1`
- » `od;`

Each L in LL is a list. For any list L, $L[i]$ is the ith element of L.

Let M denote the matrix of entries. Because M^2 contains a nonzero entry in the (i,j)-position if and only if $\sum_{r=1}^{10} M_{ir}M_{rj} \neq 0$, and because this occurs precisely when there is a flight from S_i to an intermediate state S_r from which there is a flight to S_j, it follows that the (i,j)-entry of M^2 is nonzero precisely when it is possible to get from S_i to S_j in exactly two flights. Similarly, the (i,j)-entry of M^n is nonzero precisely when it is possible to get to from S_i to S_j in (exactly) n flights.

The states in a connection-type problem need not be geographic states. An interesting example of this is obtained by considering airports as a means of connecting from one plane to another. In that case, the planes take on the role of the states. In other situations, a state might be a state of affairs or a configuration of pieces in a game.

A variation of a famous (though fairly simple) problem has a shepherd, a boat, a wolf, a sheep, and a cabbage on the left side of a river. The shepherd is to transport everything— himself, the boat, the animals, and the cabbage—to the right side. He cannot leave the wolf and the sheep or the sheep and the cabbage together unattended, and he can carry at most one occupant (in addition to himself) in the boat at one time. In this problem, a state might be represented by a list of the inhabitants of the left bank. The potential residents are the boat, the shepherd, the wolf, the sheep, and the cabbage. Of course, the boat cannot cross without the shepherd. The potential states are then S_1 = [boat, shepherd, wolf, sheep, cabbage], S_2 = [boat, shepherd, wolf, sheep], S_3 = [boat, shepherd, wolf, cabbage], S_4 = [boat, shepherd, sheep, cabbage], S_5 = [boat, shepherd, sheep], S_6 = [ ], S_7 = [cabbage], S_8 = [sheep], S_9 = [wolf], and S_{10} = [cabbage, wolf].

Another famous problem is known as the "missionary/cannibal" problem. In this problem, there are n missionaries, n cannibals and a boat on the left bank of a river. The problem is to get all $2n$ people across the river. They can cross in any order, one or two at a time—but at no time can the cannibals on either side outnumber the missionaries on that side (unless there are no missionaries on that side). Everyone is considered to be on one bank or the other—no one is counted as being in the boat. For this problem, a state might be represented by an inventory $[B,M,C]$ of the left bank, where $B = 1$ if the boat is on the left bank and 0 otherwise, M is the number of missionaries on the left bank, and C is the number of cannibals on the left bank. Following this scheme for $n = 2$ gives the legal states $S_1=[1,2,2]$, $S_2=[1,2,1]$, $S_3=[1,2,0]$, $S_4=[1,1,1]$, $S_5=[1,0,2]$, $S_6=[1,0,1]$, $S_7 = [1,0,0]$ (unattainable but legal), $S_8=[0,2,2]$ (unattainable but legal), $S_9=[0,2,1]$, $S_{10}=[0,2,0]$, $S_{11}=[0,1,1]$, $S_{12}=[0,0,2]$, $S_{13}=[0,0,1]$ and $S_{14}=[0,0,0]$. S_1 is the initial state, and the object is to get to S_{14}. In this case, you can probably find a solution in your head more easily than with a computer. For larger values of n, the problem is more difficult.

Problems on Incidence Matrices

1. Enter the incidence matrix S of the shepherd, boat, and wolf problem mentioned previously.
   a. Determine the smallest number of crossings in which the deed can be done—if, indeed, it can be done.
   b. Explain why the incidence matrix is symmetric.
2. Construct the incidence matrix of the missionary/cannibal problem for $n = 2$.
   a. Determine the minimum number of one-way trips required to get all four missionaries and cannibals across the river—if it is possible.

b. Determine a strategy for getting all four across the river (without breaking the rules, of course).

3. Repeat Problem 2 for $n = 3$ (this will take a bit longer).

4. Repeat Problem 2 for $n = 4$ (this will take quite a bit longer). There are twenty-six states. If S_0 is the initial state and S_{26} is the desired terminal state, the incidence matrix M can be obtained using the following list LR of paths from the left bank to the right bank, and the fact that M is symmetric.

$$LR = [[1,15], [1,16], [1,19], [2,16], [2,17], [2,19], [3,17], [3,18],$$
$$[3,20], [4,18], [6,20], [7,21], [8,25], [8,26], [9,23], [9,24],$$
$$[10,24], [10,25], [11,25], [11,26], [12,26]]$$

The quickest code (though it will still take quite some time to execute, perhaps thirty minutes or more, depending on your computer) is as follows:

```
•  M;
•  for i to 25
»  do
»     (" + 1)&*M;
»     od;
•  evalm(");
```

The form of the expression obtained from the first four commands is called *Horner form.* It decreases the number of matrix multiplications to twenty-six from the 325 used by the form $\sum\limits_{i=1}^{26} M^i$.

5. Enter the incidence matrix of the airline problem (described at the beginning of this section) into your *Maple* session.

a. Determine the minimum number of flights required to get a passenger from S_3 to S_7.

A question of potential interest to a traveler in the region served by this airline is whether it is possible to travel between every pair of states. Because all entries of the matrix M (and therefore of all its powers) are nonnegative, it is possible to get from state i to state j with, say, five or fewer flights if and only if the (i,j)-entry of the matrix $\sum\limits_{i=1}^{5} M^i$ is nonzero. Although it might appear to be a potentially infinite problem to determine if it is possible to travel between every pair of states, it turns out that the $(n+1)$st power of an $n \times n$ matrix A can always be written in the form

$$A^{n+1} = a_1A + a_2A^2 + \cdots + a_nA^n$$

This follows from the fact that A is a root of the polynomial generated by the *Maple* command `det(x*Id - A)`, as can be verified with the code

- `det(x*Id - A);`
- `subs(x=A,");`
- `evalm(");`

This result—known as the Cayley-Hamilton Theorem—implies that it is only necessary to sum the first ten powers of M to determine if a connection is possible.

b. Determine if it is possible to travel between every pair of states (you may want to use the `sum` command).

c. If it is possible to travel between every pair of states, determine the largest number of flights required to travel between two states.

Coding Theory

Coding theory, as you may well know, is used for a variety of purposes relating to the security of information. We are interested in a scheme to encode information so that only someone knowing the code can decipher a message.

Let us begin by assigning the numbers from 1 to 26 to the letters of the alphabet. No fancy scheme is necessary here; we can just use 1 for A, 2 for B, and so forth. So that our code is suitable for transmitting somewhat literate messages, we will also assign 0 to the space character, 27 to the period, and 28 to the question mark. We could add more punctuation marks, but the space, period, and question mark will suffice for our example. The entire translation table follows.

Translation Table

0	1	2	3	4	5	6	7	8	9
' '	A	B	C	D	E	F	G	H	I
10	11	12	13	14	15	16	17	18	19
J	K	L	M	N	O	P	Q	R	S
20	21	22	23	24	25	26	27	28	
T	U	V	W	X	Y	Z	.	?	

Let's agree to use a 5×5 matrix encoding matrix CodeMtx for the problem. The matrix CodeMtx must be invertible because CodeMtx^{-1} will be used to decode the message. Because the coding matrix is 5×5, the message matrix MsgMtx will have to be $5 \times n$ so that the product CodeMtx $\times$ MsgMtx can be formed. This requires that the number of characters in the message be a multiple of five; the message can be padded with spaces, so this is not a problem.

For example, consider the message

WHAT IS THE OPENING LINE OF MOBY DICK?

This message generates the 5×8 message matrix

$$MsgMtx = \begin{bmatrix} W & H & A & T & & I & S & \\ T & H & E & & O & P & E & N \\ I & N & G & & L & I & N & E \\ & O & F & & M & O & B & Y \\ & D & I & C & K & ? & & \end{bmatrix}$$

When translated to numeric form, using the translation table, you get the following numeric message matrix.

$$NMsgMtx = \begin{bmatrix} 23 & 8 & 1 & 20 & 0 & 9 & 19 & 0 \\ 20 & 8 & 5 & 0 & 15 & 16 & 5 & 14 \\ 9 & 14 & 7 & 0 & 12 & 9 & 14 & 5 \\ 0 & 15 & 6 & 0 & 13 & 15 & 2 & 25 \\ 0 & 4 & 9 & 3 & 11 & 28 & 0 & 0 \end{bmatrix}$$

The coded numerical message matrix is now given by

CMsgMtx = CodeMtx × NMsgMtx

The recipient can decode the message by first computing $CodeMtx^{-1} \times$ CMsgMtx to obtain NMsgMtx, and then using the translation table to obtain MsgMtx.

The message matrix can be easily defined as follows. (This will not work if any of the uppercase letters of the alphabet are assigned. You may want to begin a fresh session.)

Assign names to the punctuation marks.

- s:=` `; p:=`.`;
- q:=`?`;

The seldom-used back quotes (`) are required to define the space and punctuation marks; be sure to use a space in the definition of s.

Make a list of the characters that will be used.	• `CharLst:=` » `[s,A,B,C,D,E,F,G,H,I,J,K,L,M,N,O,` » `P,Q,R,S,T,U,V,W,X,Y,Z,p,q];`
Make a list of the message (padded out to forty characters).	• `MsgLst:=` » `[W,H,A,T,s,I,S,s,` » `T,H,E,s,O,P,E,N,` » `I,N,G,s,L,I,N,E,` » `s,O,F,s,M,O,B,Y,` » `s,D,I,C,K,q,s,s];` Check *Maple*'s output to be sure that you get the desired result.
Define the message matrix.	• `MsgMtx:=matrix(5,8,MsgLst);`

The translation of the message from alphabetic to numeric or numeric to alphabetic form can be automated as follows.

This defines a function Alpha that converts numeric data to alphabetic data.	• `for i from 0 to 28` » `do` » `  Alpha(i):=CharLst[i+1]` » `od;`
This defines a function Numeric that converts alphabetic data to numeric data.	• `for i from 0 to 28` » `do` » `  Numeric(Alpha(i)):=i` » `od;` Note that Numeric is the functional inverse of Alpha.
You can obtain NMsgMtx *by mapping* Numeric *onto* MsgMtx.	• `NMsgMtx:=map(Numeric,MsgMtx);`
Conversely, the recipient can recapture MsgMtx *by mapping* Alpha *onto* NMsgMtx.	• `map(Alpha,NMsgMtx);`

Problems on Coding Theory

In the following, assume CodeMtx is the 5×5 matrix $[c_{ij}]$ with $c_{ij} = \min(i,j)$.

1. Use CodeMtx to encode the message treated in the example.
2. Use CodeMtx to decipher the message contained in the following coded numeric message matrix.

$$
\text{CMsgMtx} = \begin{bmatrix}
24 & 29 & 54 & 38 & 6 & 27 & 36 \\
48 & 58 & 88 & 68 & 7 & 54 & 72 \\
60 & 78 & 108 & 93 & 8 & 72 & 89 \\
72 & 98 & 128 & 118 & 9 & 90 & 106 \\
81 & 117 & 136 & 131 & 10 & 95 & 118
\end{bmatrix}
$$

3. Use the *Numeric* function and CodeMtx to encode the following message.

THIS IS THE END OF CHAPTER 1. KEEP GOING, IT GETS EVEN BETTER.

2 The Algebra of Vectors

- `with(linalg);`
- `alias(Id=&*());`

In *Maple*, all matrices—including $n \times 1$ and $1 \times n$ matrices—require two indices to address their entries.

You use two subscripts to address any matrix entry— even if the matrix appears one-dimensional.

- `B:=matrix(1,4,[1,2,3,4]);`
- `B[1];`

Error messages are frequently difficult to decipher. Here, the "bounds" restrict the index to being a sequence i, j of two integers with $i = 1$ and $1 \leq j \leq 4$.

2.1 Introduction to Vectors in *Maple*

The `backsub` command returns a one-dimensional array known in *Maple* as a *vector*. In many ways, vectors are like matrices, but they require only a single index to address their entries.

2.1.1 Defining Vectors in *Maple*
[`vector`]

You define a vector in *Maple* with the `vector` command, which has several variations and options (these are detailed in the `vector` help page). Two common forms are

- `vector(n,[...])`
- `vector(n,f)`

This defines the vector $\mathbf{u} = (0,2,3)$ *using a list.*

- `u:=vector(3,[0,2,3]);`

The first argument is the length of the vector; the second argument is the list of the components.

In this case, the specification of the length of the vector is optional.

- `vector([0,2,3]);`

This is analogous to omitting the dimensions in the "list-of-lists" form of the `matrix` command.

This uses a generating function to define the 3-vector $\mathbf{v} = (v_i)$ with $v_i = \dfrac{2^i}{i}$.

- `v:=vector(3,i->2^i/i);`

Again, the first argument is the length of the vector; the second is the generating function. Note that the expression `2^i/i` does not evaluate to 2^1.

You can also use named functions to define vectors.

- `w:=vector(5,exp);`

In this case, the second argument is the function $\exp(x) = e^x$.

Reviewing and Editing Vector Definitions

Maple does not respond to a vector name by displaying the vector in standard form.

- `u;`

Consistency is a virtue.

You use the `evalm` command to tell Maple to display the standard form of a vector.

- `evalm(u);`

All vectors are displayed horizontally in *Maple*.

*The ith entry of a vector **u** is denoted u[i] in Maple.*

- `u[1];`

Notice that *Maple* has returned the value of the first component of **v**.

*To modify an entry, you simply reassign it. This changes the first component of **u** to 1.*

- `u[1]:=1;`

You may wish to use `evalm` again to verify the change.

2.1.2   Vector Arithmetic
`[ +, -, *, innerprod, angle, norm, crossprod, add, scalarmul ]`

Maple uses the same notation for addition, subtraction, and scalar multiplication of vectors as it does for matrices. This notation is summarized in Table 2.1. As with matrices, you use `evalm` to get the fully evaluated, standard form of any vector expression involving these functions.

You use `evalm` to get the evaluated standard form of the result of a vector calculation.

- `x:=2*u + v;`
- `y:=3*x - 5*u;`
- `evalm(y);`

*You can use the `print` command to see the expression defining **y** in unevaluated form.*

- `print(y);`

Note that the form of **y** has been simplified somewhat.

Table 2.1 The `evalm` Functions of Vectors[1]

Operation	Standard notation	*Maple* notation
Addition	$\mathbf{u} + \mathbf{v}$	u + v
Subtraction	$\mathbf{u} - \mathbf{u}$	u - v
Scalar multiplication	$k\mathbf{u}$	k*u
		u*k
	$\dfrac{1}{k}\mathbf{u}$	1/k*u
		u/k

Although vectors are printed horizontally in *Maple*, they are inherently neither rows nor columns—perhaps they are best thought of as *n*-tuples written horizontally to conserve screen space.

You use the `innerprod` *function to compute the Euclidean inner product* $\langle\mathbf{u},\mathbf{v}\rangle$ *of vectors.*

- `innerprod(u,v);`

Recall that for vectors in $\Re^n$, the Euclidean inner product is given by

$$\langle\mathbf{u},\mathbf{v}\rangle = \sum_{i=1}^{n} u_i v_i .$$

*The inner product A**v** of a matrix A and a vector **v** is the vector of inner products of the rows of A with **v**.*

- `A:=matrix(5,3,max);`
- `innerprod(A,v);`

You might wish to compare the entries to the inner products $\langle\mathbf{r}_i,\mathbf{v}\rangle$ of the rows $\mathbf{r}_i$ of A with $\mathbf{v}$.

*The inner product of a vector **w** and a matrix A is the vector of inner products of w with the columns of A.*

- `innerprod(w,A);`

You might wish to compare the entries to the inner products $\langle\mathbf{w},\mathbf{c}_i\rangle$ of $\mathbf{w}$ with the columns of A.

You can also use `&*` *to denote the inner product A**v** of a matrix and a vector.*

- `evalm(A &* v);`

This is equivalent to `innerprod(A,v)`.

However, you cannot use `&*` *to obtain the inner product **w**A of a vector and a matrix.*

- `evalm(w &* A);`

If expressions such as w `&*` A were allowed, `&*` would be nonassociative.

---

[1]Alternatively, you can use `add` and `scalarmul`. Use `?add` and `?scalarmul` for information.

You can use the norm *function to determine the length of the vector in the specified norm. Type* ?norm *for a discussion of available norms.*

- norm(u,2);

The second argument (2) specifies the norm

$$\|\mathbf{u}\| = \sqrt{\sum_{i=1}^{n} u_i^2} \ .$$

Other norms are available for special purposes.

You can use the angle *function to determine the angle between the vectors* **u** *and* **v**.

- angle(u,v);

Recall that the Euclidean inner product $\langle \mathbf{u}, \mathbf{v} \rangle$ is given by $\langle \mathbf{u}, \mathbf{v} \rangle = \|\mathbf{u}\| \|\mathbf{v}\| \cos(\varphi)$, where φ is the angle between **u** and **v**.

You use the crossprod *function to compute the cross product* **u** × **v** *of vectors.*

- c:=crossprod(u,v);

Recall that for vectors in $\Re^3$, the crossproduct $\mathbf{c} = \mathbf{u} \times \mathbf{v}$ satisfies $\langle \mathbf{c}, \mathbf{u} \rangle = \langle \mathbf{c}, \mathbf{v} \rangle = 0$.

2.1.3 "Cutting and Pasting" Vectors and Matrices [row, col, stack]

Define the matrix A for use as an example.

- A:=matrix(5,3,(i,j)->a.i.j);

The rows and columns of *A* are naturally associated with vectors—the row and column vectors of *A*.

Use the col *command to extract the column vectors, the* row *command to extract the row vectors.*

- S:=seq(col(A,i),i=1..3);

This lists the sequence of column vectors of *A*. The row vectors can be obtained similarly with the row command. Both the row and column vectors print in horizontal form.

You can use augment *to form a matrix with a given sequence of column vectors.*

- augment(S);

The vectors are treated here as if they were column matrices. When augment is applied to a single vector, the vector is converted into a column matrix.

You use stack *for row vectors in a fashion analogous to* augment *for column vectors.*

- stack(S);

The vectors are treated here as if they were row matrices.

You can also use augment *and* stack *to convert a vector to a column or row matrix.*

- u:=vector([1,2,3]);
- augment(u);
- stack(u);

These functions can be used with any number of conformable matrices and vectors.

You can also use matrix
to convert a vector to a
column or row matrix.

- matrix(3,1,u);
- matrix(1,3,u);

Note that the dimensions of the result must be specified when matrix is used for this purpose.

2.1.4 Solving Linear Matrix/Vector Equations

If A is an $m \times n$ matrix and $\mathbf{b}$ an m-vector, then there may exist vectors $\mathbf{x}$ for which $A\mathbf{x} = \mathbf{b}$. The solutions, if any, can be found by applying Gaussian elimination and back-substitution to the augmented matrix $[A, \mathbf{b}]$.

Define A and **b** *for use as*
an example.

- A:=matrix(5,4,(i,j)->i+j);
- b:=vector(5,i->i);

You can solve the matrix/
vector equation A**x** = **b** *by*
applying Gaussian elimina-
tion and back-substitution to
the augmented matrix [A,**b**].

- A_b:=augment(A,b);
- gausselim(A_b);
- g:=backsub(");

The vector $\mathbf{g}$ is the most general solution. All solutions are obtained from $\mathbf{g}$ by specifying the values of the parameters t3 and t4.

You can check that **g** *is a*
solution by computing the
product A**g**.

- evalm(A &* g);

A matrix/vector equation of the form $\mathbf{x}A = \mathbf{b}$ can be solved using the transpose function. Since vectors are orientation independent in *Maple*, $\mathbf{x}A = \mathbf{b}$ is equivalent to $A^T\mathbf{x} = \mathbf{b}$.

A matrix equation of the form $AX = B$ can be solved by solving each of the equations $A\mathbf{x} = \mathbf{b}_i$ separately, where $\mathbf{b}_i$ is the ith column vector of B. If $\mathbf{s}_i$ is the solution of $A\mathbf{x} = \mathbf{b}_i$, then $S = [\mathbf{s}_1, ..., \mathbf{s}_n]$ is the solution of $AX = B$, where n is the number of columns of B. The following demonstrates this technique.

Define a matrix B.

- B:=matrix(5,3,(i,j)->j+1);

The matrix B is 5×3.

Solve the three equations A**x**
= **b**$_i$ *and* augment *the*
solution vectors.

- for i to 3 do
»   augment(A,col(B,i)):
»   rref("):
»   s[i]:=backsub("):
» od:
» S:=augment(s[1],s[2],s[3]);

S is the solution. However, note that the parameters in the three columns of S are not to be considered the same—i.e., the t3's in the three columns are independent of one another, as are the t4's.

The equation $AX = B$ can also be solved by row-reducing the matrix $[A,B]$. In this case, if $[A,B]$ row-reduces to $[F,C]$, backsub is applied to $[F,C_i]$ for each column C_i of C. The following demonstrates this alternative technique.

Augment A by B and row-reduce.

- augment(A,B);
- R:=rref(");
- F:=submatrix(R,1..5,1..4);

It is tempting to use E for a reduced row echelon form. However, E is a reserved constant in the first release of *Maple V*, and *Maple* will not allow it. (Try it—if you have a later release, you may be able to use E.)

This computes the solution vectors and the solution matrix.

- for i to 3 do
- »   augment(F,col(R,4+i));
- »   s[i]:=backsub(");
- » od;
- » S:=augment(s[1],s[2],s[3]);

As in the first approach, the parameters in the three columns are not to be considered the same.

The Solutions of a Homogeneous Linear System

A linear system of the form $Ax = 0$ is said to be homogeneous. The general solution s_g of any linear system $Ax = b$ can always be written in the form $s_g = s_p + s_h$, where s_h is the general solution of the homogeneous linear system $Ax = 0$ and s_p is any particular solution of the equation $Ax = b$ (verify this statement). Consider the following example. (Note that for small matrices, it is quicker to do this by hand.)

Enter the coefficient matrix A.

- A:=matrix(5,7,(i,j)->i+j);

This is a matrix for which the system $Ax = 0$ has nontrivial solutions.

Here is a vector for which the equation Ax = b has a solution. You can use row reduction and back-substitution to obtain s_g.

- b:=vector([35,42,49,56,63]);
- s[g]:=backsub(rref(augment(A,b)));

You can check the solution by computing the product As_g.

You can get a particular solution by assigning values to all the parameters t_i in s_p. In this case, $t_i = 0, i = 1 \ldots 7$ works fine.

- Eqns:={seq(t.i=0,i=1..7)};
- s[p]:=subs(Eqns,evalm(s[g]));

This sets $t_i = 0, i = 1 \ldots 7$, in s_p. The substitutions for t_1 and t_2 have no effect.

You can obtain the general solution $\mathbf{s}_h$ of the homogeneous system either by subtracting $\mathbf{s}_p$ from $\mathbf{s}_g$ or by direct calculation.

- `augment(A,vector(5,0));`
- `rref(");`
- `s[h]:=backsub(");`
- `evalm(s[g]-s[p]);`

Compare the two results.

Note that $\mathbf{s}_g = \mathbf{s}_h + \mathbf{s}_p$.

EXERCISES 2.1 _____

1. Enter the following vectors in your *Maple* session.
   a. The 5-vector $\mathbf{u} = (u_i)$ defined by $u_i = i!$.
   b. The 5-vector $\mathbf{v} = (v_i)$ defined by $v_i = i^i$.
   c. The 5-vector $\mathbf{w} = (w_i)$ defined by $w_i = (-1)^i$.
2. Using the vectors of Exercise 1,
   a. compute the inner product of $\mathbf{u}$ and $\mathbf{v}$.
   b. compute the norm, ‖$\mathbf{u}$‖, of $\mathbf{u}$.
   c. verify the triangle inequality ‖$\mathbf{u} - \mathbf{w}$‖ ≤ ‖$\mathbf{u} - \mathbf{v}$‖ + ‖$\mathbf{v} - \mathbf{w}$‖.
   d. verify the Cauchy-Schwarz inequality $|\langle\mathbf{u},\mathbf{v}\rangle|$ ≤ ‖$\mathbf{u}$‖‖$\mathbf{v}$‖.
3. Let $A = [a_{ij}]$ be the 3×5 matrix defined by the equation $a_{ij} = \max(i,j)$. Let $\mathbf{u} = (u_i)$ be the 3-vector defined by $u_i = i!$, and let $\mathbf{v} = v_i$ be the 5-vector defined by $v_i = (-1)^i$. Determine which of the following are defined, and evaluate those that are.
   a. $\mathbf{u}A$ b. $A\mathbf{u}$ c. $\mathbf{v}A$ d. $A\mathbf{v}$
4. Let A and $\mathbf{u}$ be defined as in Exercise 3. Find all solutions of the equation $A\mathbf{x} = \mathbf{u}$.
5. Let $\mathbf{u}$ be the 3-vector $\mathbf{u} = (1,2,3,4,5)$, and let A be defined as in Exercise 3. Use `augment`, `rref`, and `backsub` to find all solutions of the equation $\mathbf{x}A = \mathbf{u}$.
6. Define a function `&.` by `'&.':=proc(x,y) innerprod(x,y) end;`. Give an example in which A and B are square matrices and `(A &. u) &. B ≠ A &.(u &. B)`. (Note: `&.` must be followed by a space or a left parenthesis.)
7. If A is a nonsingular matrix, the unique solution of the equation $AX = I$ is A^{-1}. Use row-reduction to find the inverse of the 5×5 matrix A with (i,j)-entry $a_{ij} = \max(i,j)$. Multiply A and your answer to verify your solution.
8. For any vector $\mathbf{a} = (a_1, ..., a_n)$, denote by A the row matrix $A = [a_1, ..., a_n]$. Then the two vectors

$$\mathbf{a} = (a_1, a_2, ..., a_n) \quad \text{and} \quad \mathbf{x} = (x_1, x_2, ..., x_n)$$

are orthogonal (have inner product zero) if and only if the product of the row matrix $A = [a_1, a_2, ..., a_n]$ and the vector $\mathbf{x}$ is zero. It follows that the set of all vectors orthogonal to a given vector $\mathbf{a}$ is the solution set of the homogeneous linear system $A\mathbf{x} = \mathbf{0}$. Use `stack`, augment, rref, and backsub to obtain a parametric description of all vectors **x** orthogonal to the vector **a** = (1,2,3,4,5). (This set is known as the orthogonal complement of **a**.)

9. If M is any matrix, the set of vectors **x** satisfying $M\mathbf{x} = \mathbf{0}$ is the set of vectors orthogonal to *all* rows of M. Find a parametric description of all vectors **x** orthogonal to all the rows of the 3×7 matrix $M = [m_{ij}]$, where $m_{ij} = i - j$. Note the relation of the rank of M, the width of M, and the number of parameters in the solution. Experimentally determine if a similar relationship holds for other matrices. Can you explain this?

10. It is sometimes desirable to define a family of related vectors at one time. This is conveniently done with a loop in *Maple*. Recall that in *Maple* loops have the form

> for *count* [from *start*] [by *inc*] to *finish*
>> do
>>> stuff to do
>> od;

where *start* and *finish* are the beginning and ending values of the counter *count*, which can be any variable. The "from *start*" and "by *inc*" clauses are optional; if either is not specified, *Maple* will use a default value of one.

Maple uses a default value of 1 if start *is not specified.*

```
• for i by 2 to 15
»   do
»     u[i]:=vector(3,j->i)
»   od;
```
If u has a value from earlier in the session, you may need to unassign it (explain why).

A default value of 1 is also used if inc *is not specified.*

```
• for i from 5 to 10
»   do
»     u[i]:=vector(3,j->i)
»   od;
```
Use a loop to define the collection $\{\mathbf{w}_i\}_{i=1}^{24}$ of 12-vectors where the jth component of $\mathbf{w}_i$ is i^j.

11. You can use the t1, t2, . . . subscripting style used by backsub if you wish. In particular, you may need to use it to substitute values for the variables t1, t2, . . . returned by backsub. For instance, assume you have defined the arrays A, **b**, **g** as follows.

```
• f:=proc(i,j)
» if i+j = 2 or i+j mod 2 = 1 then 0
```

```
»  else 1 fi
»  end;
•  A:=matrix(2,5,f);
•  b:=vector(2,1);
•  g:=backsub(rref(augment(A,b)));
```

To obtain a particular solution, you substitute numerical values for the parameters t1, t4, and t5 in g. You can do this easily with subs. For example, to substitute t1=3, t4=7, and t5=12, you can proceed as follows.

This makes the substitutions t1=3, t4=7, t5=12.

```
•  S:=[1,4,5];
•  V:=[3,7,12];
•  T:={seq(cat(t,S[i])=V[i],
»  i=1..3)};
•  subs(T,evalm(g));
```

Here, S is the list of "subscripts," V the list of values, and T the set of substitutions. The function cat used in the definition concatenates t and $S[i]$ to get t1, t4, and t5. The expression evalm(g) is used so that the substitution is made into the entries of **g** rather than into the expression "g".

12. Let $A = [a_{ij}]$ be the 5×11 matrix defined by $a_{ij} = \min(i,j)$. Find the general, parameterized solution $\mathbf{s}_g$ of the matrix/vector equation $A\mathbf{x}=\mathbf{b}$, $\mathbf{b} = (1,2,3,4,5)$. Write $\mathbf{s}_g$ in the form $\mathbf{s}_g = \mathbf{s}_h + \mathbf{s}_p$, where $\mathbf{s}_p$ is a particular solution of the linear system $A\mathbf{x} = \mathbf{b}$, and $\mathbf{s}_h$ is the general solution of the homogeneous linear system $A\mathbf{x} = \mathbf{0}$.

13. Let $A = [a_{ij}]$ be the 5×7 matrix defined by $a_{ij} = i/(i + j)$. Find the general, parameterized solution $\mathbf{s}_h$ of the matrix/vector equation $A\mathbf{x}=\mathbf{0}$. Write $\mathbf{s}_h$ as a sum of the form $k_1\mathbf{v}_1 + k_2\mathbf{v}_2$.

2.2 Span and Linear Independence
[linsolve]

One of the fundamental problems of vector spaces is the determination of the vectors **u** that are linear combinations of a given set $\{\mathbf{v}_1, \mathbf{v}_2, ..., \mathbf{v}_s\}$ of vectors. The set $\left\{ \sum_{i=0}^{s} k_i\mathbf{v}_i \right\}$ of all such vectors is called the *span* or *lin* of $\{\mathbf{v}_1, \mathbf{v}_2, ..., \mathbf{v}_s\}$. In *n*-space, you can determine if a given vector **u** lies in the span of vectors $\mathbf{v}_1, \mathbf{v}_2, ..., \mathbf{v}_s$ by using the augment, rref, and backsub commands. The key is that a vector **u** is a linear combination of vectors $\mathbf{v}_1, \mathbf{v}_2, ..., \mathbf{v}_s$ if and only if the vector/matrix equation $[\mathbf{v}_1, \mathbf{v}_2, ..., \mathbf{v}_s]\mathbf{x} = \mathbf{u}$ has a solution. The technique is easily applied by hand in smaller problems.

This defines a collection {$\mathbf{v}_i$} of 10-vectors using a loop.[2]

```
• for i to 12
» do
»   v[i]:=
»     vector(10,j->i/(1+(i+j mod 5)))
» od;
```

If you get an error message here, unassign the name "*v*" and enter the command again; if you are not in a new session, either name may have a conflicting definition.

Here is a vector that may lie in the span of the vectors $\mathbf{v}_i$.

```
• u:=vector(10,1);
```

Note that you cannot use **v** for the name of this vector without destroying the definitions of **v**[*i*].

This shows that $\mathbf{u}$ is a linear combination of the vectors $\mathbf{v}_i$ and returns the vector of coefficients.

```
• M:=augment(seq(v[i],i=1..12));
• augment(M,u);
• rref(");
• a:=backsub(");
```

If $\mathbf{a} = (a_i)$ then $\mathbf{u} = \displaystyle\sum_{i=1}^{12} a_i \mathbf{v}_i$.

You can easily check the solution.

```
• i:='i';
• sum(a[i]*v[i],i=1..12);
• evalm(");
```

Note that the expression evaluates to **u**, as it should.

Here a second vector $\mathbf{w}$ is checked to see if it lies in the span of {$\mathbf{v}_i$}.

```
• w:=vector(10,i->i^2);
• augment(M,w);
• rref(");
• backsub(");
```
[3]

Notice how *Maple* informs you that you have an inconsistent system.

Recall that a sequence $\mathbf{v}_1$, $\mathbf{v}_2$, ..., $\mathbf{v}_s$ of vectors is linearly independent if the only solution of the homogeneous system [$\mathbf{v}_1$, $\mathbf{v}_2$, ..., $\mathbf{v}_s$]$\mathbf{x} = \mathbf{0}$ is the trivial one, $\mathbf{x} = \mathbf{0}$. You can use the technique of the previous example to determine this.

This returns all solutions of the equation [$\mathbf{v}_1$,...,$\mathbf{v}_{12}$]$\mathbf{x}$ = $\mathbf{0}$.

```
• M:=augment(seq(v[i],i=1..12));
• augment(M,vector(10,0));
• rref(");
• backsub(");
```

In this case, the vectors are linearly dependent.

---

[2]*m* mod *n* is the remainder on dividing *m* by *n*. For example, 7 mod 5 is 2, 8 mod 5 is 3, and 10 mod 5 is 0.

[3]This sequence of operations is used so often that *Maple* has a command for it: `linsolve`. In this case you could use `linsolve(M,u);` .

This checks the linear independence of $\mathbf{v}_1, ..., \mathbf{v}_5$.

- `N:=augment(seq(v[i],i=1..5));`
- `augment(N,vector(10,0));`
- `rref(");`
- `backsub(");`

In this case, the vectors are linearly independent.

EXERCISES 2.2 _____

1. Determine if the vector $\mathbf{b} = (1,2,3,4,5)$ lies in the span of the following sets of vectors.
   a. $\mathbf{v}_1 = (5,4,3,2,1)$, $\mathbf{v}_2 = (4,3,2,1,5)$, $\mathbf{v}_3 = (3,2,1,5,4)$
   b. $\mathbf{v}_1 = (2,3,4,5,6)$, $\mathbf{v}_2 = (3,4,5,6,7)$
2. Determine if the vector $\mathbf{b} = (1,1,1,1,1)$ lies in the span of the following sets of vectors.
   a. $\mathbf{v}_1 = (5,4,3,2,1)$, $\mathbf{v}_2 = (1,2,3,4,5)$, $\mathbf{v}_3 = (3,2,1,5,4)$
   b. $\mathbf{v}_1 = (2,3,4,5,6)$, $\mathbf{v}_2 = (8,7,6,5,4)$, $\mathbf{v}_3 = (1,0,1,0,1)$
3. Determine if the 15-vector $\mathbf{v} = (v_i)$ defined by $v_i = i$ lies in the span of the 15-vectors $\mathbf{w}_i$, $i = 1..15$, where the jth component w_{ij} of $\mathbf{w}_i$ is given by $w_{ij} = i - j$. Do the same for the vector $\mathbf{v} = (v_i)$ defined by $v_i = i^2$.

In Exercises 4–7, use the 10-vectors $\mathbf{v}_i = (v_{ij})$ defined by $v_{ij} = 1/(1+(i - j \bmod 5))$, $i = 1...10$.

4. Determine if the vectors $\mathbf{v}_1, \mathbf{v}_2, ..., \mathbf{v}_{10}$ are linearly independent.
5. Determine if any of the vectors $\mathbf{v}_1, \mathbf{v}_2, ..., \mathbf{v}_{10}$ is a linear combination of preceding vectors.
6. Repeat Exercise 4 for $\mathbf{v}_1, \mathbf{v}_2, ..., \mathbf{v}_5$.
7. Determine if any of the vectors $\mathbf{v}_1, \mathbf{v}_2, ..., \mathbf{v}_5$ is a linear combination of preceding vectors.

2.3 Bases, Dimension, and Coordinates
[nops, basis]

As you may recall, a linearly independent spanning set for a vector space V is called a *basis*. You can obtain a basis for a subspace of n-space from a spanning set by row-reduction. The set of linear combinations of the rows of an $m \times n$ matrix A is a subspace of $\mathfrak{R}^n$. It is called the row space of A. The key to the following is that the row space is not changed by elementary row operations (verify this).

This generates the required vectors $\mathbf{v}_i$. *Their definitions may still be active from the previous section.*

- `for i to 12`
- » `do`
- » `  v[i]:=vector(10,j->i/(1+(i+j mod 5)))`
- » `od;`

You can find a basis by stacking the vectors into a matrix and row-reducing.

- `M:=stack(seq(v[i],i=1..12));`
- `G:=gausselim(");`

The five nonzero rows form a basis for the subspace spanned by v_1, v_2, ..., v_{10}, but they do not form a subset of $\{v_1, v_2, ..., v_5\}$.

The following extracts a basis from the row-reduced matrix.

Recall that the number of nonzero rows of the matrix is its rank.

- `seq(row(G,i),i=1..rank(G));`
- `B:={"};`

You may recall that a sequence v_1, v_2, ..., v_n of vectors is linearly independent if and only if $v_1 \neq 0$ and no v_i is a linear combination of v_1, ..., v_{i-1} (or, equivalently, none is a linear combination of those after it). It is obvious by this criterion that the vectors in B are linearly independent: no element is a linear combination of following elements (if the order is reversed, no element is a linear combination of preceding elements).

You can easily tell which (if any) of a sequence of vectors is a linear combination of preceding terms of the sequence by applying augment and rref to the sequence. A vector v_i is a linear combination of vectors v_1, v_2, ..., v_{i-1} if and only if the reduced row echelon form G of the matrix $[v_1, v_2, ..., v_n]$ has a first nonzero entry (in some row) in the ith-column. Noting that, it follows that if the first nonzero entries of the rows of G appear in columns i_1, ..., i_s, then v_{i_1}, ..., v_{i_s} are a basis for the subspace spanned by v_1, v_2, ..., v_n.

Consider the previous example v_1, v_2, ..., v_{12} once again.

Use augment to place the vectors in a matrix as columns.

- `augment(seq(v[i],i=1..12));`

Now, row-reduce the matrix.

- `R:=rref(");`

By inspection, each of v_6, ..., v_{12} is a linear combination of preceding vectors, and none of v_1, ..., v_5 is a linear combination of preceding vectors. It follows that v_1, ..., v_5 is a basis for the subspace spanned by v_1, ..., v_{12}.[4]

In some cases you may wish to have *Maple* count the number of elements of a set—perhaps to find the dimension of a subspace by counting the number of vectors in a basis. This can be particularly helpful with subspaces of large dimension.

This gives the dimension of the subspace spanned by the vectors v_i.

- `nops(B);`

---

[4]*Maple* also has a built-in basis command that can be used to extract a basis.

Bases are used to "coordinatize" vector spaces, making it possible to proceed in an n-dimensional vector space in the same way that you would in $\Re^n$. For example, the standard basis, $\mathbf{S} = \{1, \mathbf{x}, \mathbf{x}^2, ..., \mathbf{x}^5\}$ for the vector space $\mathbf{P}_5$ of polynomials of degree five or less, associates the "coordinate vector" $(a_0, a_1, a_2, a_3, a_4, a_5)$ with the polynomial $p = a_0 + a_1\mathbf{x} + a_2\mathbf{x}^2 + a_3\mathbf{x}^3 + a_4\mathbf{x}^4 + a_5\mathbf{x}^5$. The polynomials $p_i = \mathbf{x}^i$ themselves correspond to the 6-tuples $\mathbf{e}_1 = (1,0,0,0,0,0), ..., \mathbf{e}_6 = (0,0,0,0,0,1)$. If we let $(p)_S$ denote the coordinate vector of a polynomial p, then $p = \sum_{i=1}^{k} c_i q_i$ if and only if $(p)_S = \sum_{i=1}^{k} c_i(q_i)_S$. This reduces questions about $\mathbf{P}_5$ to questions about $\Re^6$. The same technique can be used to reduce questions about any n-dimensional space to questions about $\Re^n$.

Change of Coordinates

The coordinatization that one gets from a particular basis $\mathbf{B}$ is peculiar to $\mathbf{B}$. If one works with a different basis, one gets a different coordinate system as well. The key relationship between a basis $\mathbf{B} = \{\mathbf{b}_1, \mathbf{b}_2, ..., \mathbf{b}_n\}$ and the coordinates of other vectors is given by the simple identity $B(\mathbf{v})_\mathbf{B} = \mathbf{v}$, where $B = [\mathbf{b}_1, \mathbf{b}_2, ..., \mathbf{b}_n]$. If $\mathbf{C} = \{\mathbf{c}_1, \mathbf{c}_2, ..., \mathbf{c}_n\}$ is a second basis, and if $C = [\mathbf{c}_1, \mathbf{c}_2, ..., \mathbf{c}_n]$, then $C(\mathbf{v})_\mathbf{C} = \mathbf{v}$ as well, hence $B(\mathbf{v})_\mathbf{B} = C(\mathbf{v})_\mathbf{C}$. If this is in $\Re^n$, it follows that $(\mathbf{v})_\mathbf{C} = C^{-1}B(\mathbf{v})_\mathbf{B}$. The matrix $C^{-1}B$ is called the $\mathbf{B}$ to $\mathbf{C}$ *change of coordinate matrix* or *transition matrix*. In general, the $\mathbf{B}$ to $\mathbf{C}$ change of coordinate matrix has ith column vector $(\mathbf{b}_i)_\mathbf{C}$.

Note that the reduced row echelon form of the matrix $[C,B]$ is $[I, C^{-1}B]$. This offers another procedure for finding the transition matrix.

EXERCISES 2.3 _____

1. Find bases for each of the following vector spaces.
   a. The subspace of $\Re^5$ spanned by the vectors $\{\mathbf{v}_i\}_{i=1}^{4}$, where $\mathbf{v}_i$ is the 5-vector defined by $\mathbf{v}_i = (i, i+1, i+2, i+3, i+4)$
   b. The subspace of $\Re^6$ spanned by the vectors $\{\mathbf{v}_i\}_{i=1}^{7}$, where $\mathbf{v}_i = (v_{ij})$ is the 6-vector defined by $v_{ij} = 1/(i+j)$
   c. The solution space of the linear system $A\mathbf{x} = 0$, where $A = [a_{ij}]$ is the 7×9 matrix defined by $a_{ij} = 1/(i+j-1)$

2. Determine if the polynomial $p = \sum_{j=0}^{12} \mathbf{x}^j$ is a linear combination of the polynomials $q_i = \sum_{j=0}^{12} (x-i)^j, i = 1, ..., 13$. (Note: You may wish to expand the q_i. The coefficient of $\mathbf{x}^i$ of a polynomial $q = \sum_{i=0}^{12} c_i \mathbf{x}^i$ in

expanded form is returned by the *Maple* command `coeff(q,x,i)`. For example, the coefficient of x^3 in q is given by `coeff(q,x,3)`.

3. Determine if the polynomials q_i of Exercise 2 are a basis for $\mathbf{P}_{12}$. (Note: The polynomials q_i are a basis for $\mathbf{P}_{12}$ if and only if the associated coordinate vectors $(q_i)_\mathbf{B}$ of the q_i, with respect to a basis $\mathbf{B}$, are a basis for $\mathfrak{R}^{13}$. For example, you might use the coordinates with respect to the basis $\mathbf{B} = \{1, \mathbf{x}, \mathbf{x}^2, ..., \mathbf{x}^{12}\}$.)

4. Let $B = [b_{ij}]$ be the 5×5 matrix given by $b_{ij} = \max(i,j)$. Let $C = [c_{ij}]$ be the 5×5 matrix given by $c_{ij} = \min(i,j)$. Denote the columns of B by $\mathbf{b}_1$, ..., $\mathbf{b}_5$, and the columns of C by $\mathbf{c}_1$, ..., $\mathbf{c}_5$. Let $\mathbf{B} = \{\mathbf{b}_1, ..., \mathbf{b}_5\}$ and $\mathbf{C} = \{\mathbf{c}_1, ..., \mathbf{c}_5\}$. Let $\mathbf{v} = (5,4,3,2,1)$.

   a. Find the $\mathbf{B}$-coordinates of $\mathbf{v}$ by direct calculation
   b. Find the $\mathbf{C}$-coordinates of $\mathbf{v}$ by direct calculation
   c. Find the $\mathbf{B}$ to $\mathbf{C}$ change of coordinate matrix P
   d. Find the $\mathbf{C}$ to $\mathbf{B}$ change of coordinate matrix Q
   e. Verify that $P(\mathbf{v})_\mathbf{B} = (\mathbf{v})_\mathbf{C}$
   f. Verify that $Q(\mathbf{v})_\mathbf{C} = (\mathbf{v})_\mathbf{B}$
   g. Verify that $PQ = \mathbf{I}$

2.4 Subspaces Associated with a Matrix
[rowspace, colspace, nullspace]

If A is an $m \times n$ matrix with real entries, the set of linear combinations of the row vectors of A is a subspace of $\mathfrak{R}^n$, called the row space of A. In Section 2.3, the row space was used to find a basis for a subspace of $\mathfrak{R}^n$, given a finite spanning set.

Other subspaces associated with a matrix are:

- Its column space—the collection of linear combinations of its column vectors.
- Its null space—the set of solutions of the equation $A\mathbf{x} = \mathbf{0}$.
- Its kernel—the kernel is the same as the null space.
- Its range space—the collection of vectors $\mathbf{b}$ of the form $\mathbf{b} = A\mathbf{x}$, for some $\mathbf{x}$. The range space is equal to the column space.

One of the most useful ways of describing a subspace is by giving a basis for it. In Section 2.3, you found a basis from a spanning set by row-reduction. You can use the same techniques to find bases for the row space or column space of any matrix.[5] Finding a basis for the null space is a bit more involved. Consider, once again, the example of the matrix A defined in subsection 2.1.5.

Define the matrix A.

- `A:=matrix(5,7,(i,j)->i+j);`

---

[5]*Maple* has special commands for achieving this, `rowspace` and `colspace`.

Solve the matrix/vector
equation $A\mathbf{x} = \mathbf{0}$.

- `augment(A,vector(5,0));`
- `rref(");`
- `s[h]:=backsub(");`

The vector $\mathbf{s}_h$ is the general solution.

The vector $\mathbf{s}_h$ obtained in our session was

$$(t_3 + 2\,t_4 + 3\,t_5 + 4\,t_6 + 5\,t_7, -2\,t_3 - 3\,t_4 - 4\,t_5 - 5\,t_6 - 6\,t_7, t_3, t_4, t_5, t_6, t_7),$$

which can be rewritten as $\mathbf{s}_h = t_3\,\mathbf{v}_1 + t_4\mathbf{v}_2 + t_5\mathbf{v}_3 + t_6\mathbf{v}_4 + t_7\mathbf{v}_5$, where

$\mathbf{v}_1 = (1, -2, 1, 0, 0, 0, 0)$ $\mathbf{v}_2 = (2, -3, 0, 1, 0, 0, 0)$
$\mathbf{v}_3 = (3, -4, 0, 0, 1, 0, 0)$ $\mathbf{v}_4 = (4, -5, 0, 0, 0, 1, 0)$
$\mathbf{v}_5 = (5, -6, 0, 0, 0, 0, 1)$

Here, the entries of $\mathbf{v}_1$ are the coefficients of t3, the entries of $\mathbf{v}_2$ the coefficients of t4, and so on.

The vectors $\mathbf{v}_1, \ldots, \mathbf{v}_5$ can be obtained using the *Maple* `coeff` command to pick off the coefficients of the parameters ti as follows.

- `Parms:=[t3,t4,t5,t6,t7];`
- `for i to 5 do`
- » `v[i]:=vector(7,j->coeff(s[h][j],Parms[i]))`
- » `od;`[6]

EXERCISES 2.4 _____

1. For a randomly generated 5×7 matrix A, verify that the dimension of the row space of A is equal to the dimension of the column space of A. This result is true in general, and is commonly stated in the form

   row rank = column rank

   (Use the `randmatrix` command to generate the matrix. You can use the `row` and `col` commands to extract the row vectors and column vectors.)
2. Let $f(i,j) = i + j$. For each of the following matrices, find bases for the null space, the row space and the column space.
   a. The 5×13 matrix $A = [a_{ij}]$ defined by $a_{ij} = f(i,j)$.
   b. The 11×7 matrix $A = [a_{ij}]$ defined by $a_{ij} = f(i,j)$.
   c. The 16×8 matrix $A = [a_{ij}]$ defined by $a_{ij} = f(i,j)$.
3. Each $m \times n$ matrix in Exercise 2 has a row-space basis with two vectors and a null-space basis with $n - 2$ vectors. Can this be generalized?

---

[6]*Maple* has a `nullspace` command that could be used here to obtain the same basis for the null space of the matrix.

4. Let $h(i,j) = 1/(i + j - 1)$. Find bases for the null space, row space, and column space of the $m \times n$ matrix $A = [h(i,j)]$ for each of the following cases.

    a. $m = 13, n = 15$ b. $m = 14, n = 3$ c. $m = 27, n = 5$

5. It is dangerous to assign values to the *Maple* variables t1, t2, ... used by backsub. To see why, let $A = [a_{ij}]$ be the matrix defined by $a_{ij} = i - j$. Let **z** be the zero 3-vector. Use augment, rref, and backsub to obtain the general solution of the equation $A\mathbf{x} = \mathbf{z}$. Now, assign t3 the value 0 and repeat the exercise. (Be sure to *unassign* the global variable t3 when you are finished with the exercise.)

2.5 The Gram-Schmidt Procedure
   [GramSchmidt]

Given a finite basis $\mathbf{B} = \{\mathbf{v}_1, \mathbf{v}_2, ..., \mathbf{v}_s\}$ for a vector space with an inner product, it is always possible to find an orthogonal basis $\mathbf{C} = \{\mathbf{w}_1, \mathbf{w}_2, ..., \mathbf{w}_s\}$. The technique used to do so is called the Gram-Schmidt procedure. (A set $\{\mathbf{w}_1, \mathbf{w}_2, ..., \mathbf{w}_s\}$ of vectors is said to be orthogonal if $\langle \mathbf{w}_i, \mathbf{w}_j \rangle = \mathbf{0}$ whenever $i \neq j$.)

Recall that the orthogonal projection of a vector **u** onto a vector **v** is given by $\text{proj}_\mathbf{v}(\mathbf{u}) = \dfrac{\langle \mathbf{u, v} \rangle}{\langle \mathbf{v, v} \rangle} \mathbf{v}$, where $\langle \mathbf{u,v} \rangle$ denotes the innerproduct of **u** and **v**.

The Gram-Schmidt procedure is stated inductively as follows: Given a sequence $\mathbf{v}_1, \mathbf{v}_2, ..., \mathbf{v}_s$ of vectors,

$$\mathbf{w}_1 = \mathbf{v}_1$$

$$\mathbf{w}_{i+1} = \mathbf{v}_{i+i} - \sum_{j=1}^{i} \text{proj}_{\mathbf{w}j}(\mathbf{v}_{i+1})$$

Assume, for example, you are given the collection $\{\mathbf{v}_i\}_{i=1}^{5}$ of vectors in real 7-space, where the jth component of $\mathbf{v}_i$ is $v_{ij} = \max(i,j)$. The following will produce an orthogonal basis $\mathbf{C} = \{\mathbf{w}_i\}_{i=1}^{5}$ for the subspace V spanned by the vectors $\{\mathbf{v}_i\}_{i=1}^{5}$.

This defines the vectors $\{\mathbf{v}_i\}_{i=1}^{5}$ *in the session.*

- ```
  for i to 5
  ```
- » ```
  do
  ```
- » ```
  v[i]:=vector(7,j->max(i,j))
  ```
- » ```
  od;
  ```

This verifies that $\{\mathbf{v}_i\}_{i=1}^{5}$ *is a basis for the subspace V they span.*

- ```
  augment(seq(v[i],i=1..5));
  ```
- ```
  rref(");
  ```

The result returned shows that $\mathbf{v}_1, ..., \mathbf{v}_5$ are linearly independent (each column has a nonzero entry). It follows that $\mathbf{v}_1, ..., \mathbf{v}_5$ are a basis for V.

This defines iprod(*u*,*v*) *as the Euclidean inner product of* **u** *and* **v**.

```
• iprod:=proc(x,y)
»    innerprod(x,y)
» end;
```
The macro facility could have been used here.

This defines the orthogonal projection

$$\text{proj}_{\mathbf{v}}(\mathbf{u}) = \frac{\langle \mathbf{u}, \mathbf{v} \rangle}{\langle \mathbf{v}, \mathbf{v} \rangle} \mathbf{v}$$

of a vector **u** *onto a vector* **v**.

```
• proj:=proc(u,v)
»    iprod(u,v)/iprod(v,v)*v
» end;
```
You could use `innerprod` directly here but `iprod` is shorter. Also, you can reuse this code later with a different inner product.

This defines the vectors

$$\mathbf{w}_i = \mathbf{v}_i - \sum_{j=1}^{i-1} \text{proj}_{\mathbf{w}_j}(\mathbf{v}_i).$$

```
• j:='j';
• for i to 5
» do
»   w[i]:=evalm(v[i]-
»   sum('proj(v[i],w[j])',j=1..i-1))
» od;
```
Note the single quotes around the expression to be evaluated by `sum`; they are required to force the evaluation of the expression in the correct order—a technicality of *Maple*.

You can easily check that the procedure works.

This verifies that the vectors $\{\mathbf{w}_i\}_{i=1}^{5}$ *are mutually orthogonal.*

```
• for i to 5
» do
»    for j to i-1
»    do
»     print(iprod(w[i],w[j]))
»    od
» od;
```

If, as in this case, you are using the standard Euclidean inner product on vectors containing no radicals,[7] you can also use *Maple*'s `GramSchmidt` command.

This uses Maple's built-in `GramSchmidt` *command to obtain an orthogonal basis.*

```
• G:=GramSchmidt([seq(evalm(v[i]),
» i=1..5)]);
```
The use of `evalm` here is required with `GramSchmidt` for indexed names.[8]

Note that *Maple*'s `GramSchmidt` command does not necessarily return vectors of norm one.

---

[7]Radicals are not a problem in Release 1.
[8]This is not required in Release 2.

EXERCISES 2.5 _____

1. Let $\{\mathbf{v}_i\}_{i=1}^{3}$ be the collection of 3-vectors defined by $\mathbf{v}_i = (v_{ij})$, where $v_{ij} = 1/(i + j)$. Verify that the vectors $\mathbf{v}_i$ are linearly independent, and apply the Gram-Schmidt procedure to obtain an orthogonal basis for Euclidean 3-space. Verify your answer.

2. Let $\{\mathbf{v}_i\}_{i=1}^{6}$ be the collection of 8-vectors defined by $\mathbf{v}_i = (v_{ij})$, where $v_{ij} = i/(i + j)$, and let V be the subspace spanned by $\{\mathbf{v}_i\}_{i=1}^{6}$. Verify that the vectors $\mathbf{v}_i$ are linearly independent and apply the Gram-Schmidt procedure to obtain a set of vectors that are orthogonal with respect to the Euclidean inner product. Verify your answer.

3. Use the solution from Exercise 2 to obtain a basis for V consisting of mutually orthogonal vectors, each of norm one—in other words, an orthonormal basis for V.

4. Let $\{\mathbf{v}_i\}_{i=1}^{6}$ be the collection of 8-vectors defined in Exercise 1. Define the inner product of 8-vectors $\mathbf{x} = (x_i)$ and $\mathbf{y} = (y_i)$ by $\langle \mathbf{x},\mathbf{y} \rangle = \displaystyle\sum_{i=1}^{8} i x_i y_i$.

    Apply the Gram-Schmidt procedure to the vectors $\{\mathbf{v}_i\}_{i=1}^{6}$ to obtain an orthogonal spanning set relative to the given inner product.

2.6 Applications

Stability and Steady-state Vectors

Many physical situations are nicely described by a vector of values. For example, a vector can be used to record the fraction of the customers buying each of a collection of competing brands. A situation in which a number of companies are competing for the same customers can be thought of as a dynamic system: customers can change from brand to brand depending on price, advertising, or other factors. A vector can be used to record a state of the system.

   In many cases, the forces acting on a dynamic system can be summarized in a matrix M so that the $(n + 1)$st state vector of the system can be determined from the nth state vector by the simple formula $\mathbf{s}_{n+1} = M\mathbf{s}_n$. In some particularly important cases, the system tends toward a steady state $\mathbf{s}$ satisfying $M\mathbf{s} = \mathbf{s}$. The matrix M is known as the transition matrix and the vector $\mathbf{s}$ is known as a steady-state vector.

   For example, assume two high-quality ice-cream stores, The Freezer and The Creamery, next door to each other in River City. Assume that year after year, $\dfrac{2}{3}$ of The Freezer's customers are repeat customers from the previous year, whereas $\frac{1}{3}$ of them are converts from The Creamery. At the

same time, assume that $\frac{5}{9}$ of The Creamery's customers are faithful repeat-

ers and $\frac{4}{9}$ of them are adventurous experimenters from The Freezer. In other

words, The Freezer gets $\frac{2}{3}$ of their own customers back plus $\frac{4}{9}$ of The

Creamery's customers, while The Creamery gets $\frac{5}{9}$ of their own customers

and $\frac{1}{3}$ of The Freezer's customers. If s_n is the 2-vector with $s_n[1]$ = (fraction
of all customers patronizing The Freezer in the nth year) and $s_n[2]$ = (fraction
of all customers patronizing The Creamery in the nth year), then the matrix
that gives s_{n+1} from s_n is simply

$$
M = \begin{bmatrix} \dfrac{2}{3} & \dfrac{4}{9} \\ \dfrac{1}{3} & \dfrac{5}{9} \end{bmatrix}
$$

If $s = (f, c)$, then $Ms = (\frac{2}{3} f + \frac{4}{9} c, \frac{1}{3} f + \frac{5}{9} c)$.

Note that the sum of the entries in any column of M is 1 and that all
entries are nonnegative. If the rows and columns of M are labeled F and C
(for Freezer and Creamery) in that order, then the (i,j)-entry is the fraction of
j's customers that move to i's establishment. The (F,F)-entry is the fraction
of The Freezer's customers that continue at The Freezer; the (F,C)-entry is
the fraction of The Creamery's customers that move to The Freezer; the
(C,F)-entry is the fraction of The Freezer's customers that move to The
Creamery; and the (C,C)-entry is the fraction of The Creamery's customers
that stay on at The Creamery.

Assuming both establishments have a fair start—with each getting $\frac{1}{2}$

of the potential clientele—the "initial state vector" is $s_0 = \left(\frac{1}{2}, \frac{1}{2} \right)$; the first
coordinate gives the fraction of the local ice-cream eaters who patronize The
Freezer in the first year, and the second coordinate gives the fraction of the
ice-cream eaters who patronize The Creamery in the first year.

At the end of the first year, after everyone has re-evaluated his or her
choice, the vector s_1, which gives the current state, is given by $s_1 = Ms_0$, and
so on.

This defines the initial-state vector s_0 and the transition matrix M.

- `s[0]:=vector([1/2,1/2]);`
- `M:=matrix(2,2,[2/3,4/9,1/3,5/9]);`

This gives the state of affairs at the end of the first year.

- `s[1]:=evalm(M &* s[0]);`

This does not appear to bode well for The Creamery—it lost $\left(\dfrac{1}{2} - \dfrac{4}{9}\right)\Big/\dfrac{1}{2} \approx$ 11% of its business to The Freezer.

This gives the state of affairs after two years.

- `s[2]:=evalm(M &* s[1]);`

This gives a bit rosier picture for The Creamery; it lost only $\left(\dfrac{4}{9} - \dfrac{35}{81}\right)\Big/\dfrac{4}{9} \approx 2.8\%$ of its business to The Freezer this time—certainly much better than the first year.

This gives the state of affairs for the next five years.

- `for i from 2 to 6`
- `» do`
- `»   s[i+1]:=evalm(M &* s[i])`
- `» od;`

Sometimes exact answers may not be the easiest to interpret.

This gives the same data in decimal percent form.

- `for i from 1 to 7`
- `» do`
- `»   map(100*evalf,s[i])`
- `» od;`

The Creamery might be happier with a larger share of the market, but it looks as if their future is secure; the system stabilizes at about (57%,43%). An interesting aspect of this problem is that the outcome is virtually independent of the initial state vector s_0: even if one of the businesses starts with all the customers, after three or four years the situation is still about (57%,43%).

Though this ice-cream parlor example may appear somewhat simplistic, it demonstrates a property common to such systems—they tend toward a state of equilibrium. (There exists a steady-state vector **s** satisfying $M\mathbf{s} = \mathbf{s}$ to which the s_n are converging.)

We have the tools to find the steady-state vectors. Note that the equation $M\mathbf{s} = \mathbf{s}$ is equivalent to the equation $(Id - M)\mathbf{s} = \mathbf{0}$. Hence, the steady-state vectors form the null space of the matrix $Id - M$.

This gives the space of all steady-state vectors.

- `augment(Id-M,vector(2,0));`
- `rref(");`
- `NS:=backsub(");`

Recall that 1 can be used in place of the identity matrix in a "matrix polynomial" if you prefer.

This takes a single basis vector from the subspace and scales it so that the sum of its coordinates is one.

- `t:=subs(t2=1,evalm(NS));`
- `s:=evalm(t/(t[1]+t[2]));`

You could use `"` in place of `evalm(NS)` in the definition of `t` (assuming that you define `t` immediately after you define `NS`).

Note that $s \approx (57\%, 43\%)$ and that, because of the physical constraints of the problem, it is the only possible steady-state vector of the system.

Problems on Stability and Steady-state Vectors

1. Verify that the steady-state vector of the ice-cream parlor example tends to approximately $(57\%, 43\%)$ even if
   a. The Freezer starts with all the customers, or
   b. The Creamery starts with all the customers.
2. Assume that five paint stores open in River City, all competing for the same customers. Because of price fluctuations of differing brands, customer satisfaction, and other variables, some customers try different stores, and others do not. Assume that in year $n + 1$, the fraction of store i's customers who were customers of store j in year n is given by the transition matrix

$$M = \begin{bmatrix} 2/10 & 3/10 & 2/10 & 4/10 & 2/10 \\ 3/10 & 2/10 & 1/10 & 1/10 & 2/10 \\ 1/10 & 1/10 & 3/10 & 1/10 & 2/10 \\ 3/10 & 2/10 & 3/10 & 1/10 & 3/10 \\ 1/10 & 2/10 & 1/10 & 3/10 & 1/10 \end{bmatrix}$$

Find the steady-state vector s and investigate how quickly the annual-state vectors s_n converge to it, given $s_0 = \left(\dfrac{1}{5}, \dfrac{1}{5}, \dfrac{1}{5}, \dfrac{1}{5}, \dfrac{1}{5} \right)$.

3. Let $A = [a_{ij}]$ be the 10×10 matrix given by $a_{ij} = \max(i,j)$. Let $\mathbf{d} = (d_i)$ be the 10-vector given by $d_i = \displaystyle\sum_{j=1}^{10} a_{ij}$. Let $M = [m_{ij}]$ be the matrix given by $m_{ij} = a_{ij}/d_j$. (Note that the entries of M are all positive and that the column sums are all one.) Find the steady-state vectors of M.

Orthogonal Projection
[leastsqrs, rank]

Given a subspace W of a real inner product space V and a vector $\mathbf{v}$ in V, *t*here is one vector $\mathbf{u}$ in W that is closer to $\mathbf{v}$ (as measured by the norm $\|\mathbf{u} - \mathbf{v}\| = \sqrt{\langle \mathbf{u} - \mathbf{v}, \mathbf{u} - \mathbf{v} \rangle}$) than any other vector of W. The vector $\mathbf{u}$ is chosen so that $\mathbf{v} - \mathbf{u}$ is orthogonal to W (that is, to every vector in W), and it is called the *orthogonal projection* of $\mathbf{v}$ onto W.

Recall that the orthogonal projection $\mathbf{u}$ of a vector $\mathbf{v}$ onto a vector $\mathbf{w}$ is given by the formula $\mathbf{u} = \left(\dfrac{\langle \mathbf{v}, \mathbf{w} \rangle}{\langle \mathbf{w}, \mathbf{w} \rangle} \right) \mathbf{w}$. In this case, the vector $\mathbf{v} - \mathbf{u}$ is orthogonal to both $\mathbf{w}$ and $\mathbf{u}$, and $\mathbf{v}$ is the sum of the vectors $\mathbf{u}$ and $\mathbf{v} - \mathbf{u}$. Hence, $\mathbf{u}$ is in the subspace spanned by $\mathbf{w}$, and $\mathbf{v} - \mathbf{u}$ is orthogonal to the subspace spanned by $\mathbf{w}$. If $\{\mathbf{w}_i\}_{i=1}^s$ is an orthogonal basis for W, then the orthogonal projection $\mathbf{u}$ of $\mathbf{v}$ onto W is the sum of the orthogonal projections of $\mathbf{v}$ onto the $\mathbf{w}_i$, $\mathbf{u} = \displaystyle\sum_{i=1}^s \left(\dfrac{\langle \mathbf{v}, \mathbf{w}_i \rangle}{\langle \mathbf{w}_i, \mathbf{w}_i \rangle} \right) \mathbf{w}_i$. In this case, the vector $\mathbf{v}$ is the sum of the vectors $\mathbf{u}$ and $\mathbf{v} - \mathbf{u}$, with $\mathbf{u}$ in the subspace spanned by the $\mathbf{w}_i$ and $\mathbf{v} - \mathbf{u}$ orthogonal to the subspace spanned by the $\mathbf{w}_i$.

Note that if $a_i = \dfrac{\langle \mathbf{v}, \mathbf{w}_i \rangle}{\langle \mathbf{w}_i, \mathbf{w}_i \rangle}$ for $i = 1, \ldots, s$, and if $\mathbf{a} = (a_i)$, then $[\mathbf{w}_1, \mathbf{w}_2, \ldots, \mathbf{w}_s]\mathbf{a} = \mathbf{u}$. Because $\mathbf{u}$ is the vector in W closest to $\mathbf{v}$, the vector $\mathbf{a}$ is considered an approximate solution of the matrix/vector equation $[\mathbf{w}_1, \mathbf{w}_2, \ldots, \mathbf{w}_s]\mathbf{x} = \mathbf{v}$.

Given any $m \times n$ matrix A and m-vector $\mathbf{v}$, it is possible to compute the orthogonal projection $\mathbf{u}$ of $\mathbf{v}$ onto the column space of A and then solve the equation $A\mathbf{x} = \mathbf{u}$. If A has rank n, then the solution is necessarily unique, but otherwise not (verify this). In any case, solutions of the equation $A\mathbf{x} = \mathbf{u}$ are called *least-squares solutions* of the equation $A\mathbf{x} = \mathbf{v}$. In *Maple*, you can use the leastsqrs command to obtain the general least-squares solution.

Consider the 7×5 matrix $A = [a_{ij}]$ dfined by $a_{ij} = \min(i,j)$. Let $\mathbf{v}$ be the 7-vector $\mathbf{v} = (1,2,3,4,5,6,7)$.

Define A and $\mathbf{v}$.

- A:=matrix(7,5,min);
- v:=vector(7,i->i);

The matrix A has rank 5, a fact that is easily verified.

- rank(A);

It follows that the columns of A are a basis for its column space.

You can obtain an orthogonal basis for the column space of A with the col *and* GramSchmidt *commands.*

- seq(col(A,i),i=1..5);
- B:=GramSchmidt(["]);

The vectors of the orthogonal basis can now be addressed as $B[i]$, $i = 1, \ldots, 5$.

This defines the orthogonal projection of one vector onto another (relative to the Euclidean inner product).

- `proj:=proc(x,y)`
- » `y*innerprod(x,y)/`
- » `  innerprod(y,y)`
- » `end;`

*You can now obtain the orthogonal projection of **v** onto the column space of A.*

- `i:='i';`
- `u:=evalm(sum(`
- » `'proj(v,B[i])',i=1..5));`

The variable *i* is unassigned as a precaution before using it in sum, because sum will not work with an assigned counter. The quotes around proj() are a technical necessity to force evaluation of *i* in the expression before evaluation of the expression. The necessity of quotes can often be determined only by trial.

*You can row-reduce to obtain the least squares solution **a** of the equation Ax = v.*

- `a:=backsub(rref(augment(A,u)));`

Note that solution of the equation $Ax = \mathbf{u}$ cannot be unique if the matrix A has rank less than n (verify this). The solution of least norm can be obtained by orthogonal projection onto the row space of A.[9]

You can directly obtain the least-squares solution of a matrix/vector equation $Ax = \mathbf{v}$ in *Maple* with the leastsqrs command. If desired, you can then use it to calculate the orthogonal projection of **v** onto the column space of A.

You can use Maple's leastsqrs *command to compute the least-squares solution of a matrix/vector equation Ax = v.*

- `u:=leastsqrs(A,v);`

This works even if there is no exact solution. Note that the orthogonal projection of **v** onto the column space of A is given by $A\mathbf{u}$. Hence, $A\mathbf{u}$ is the vector closest to **v** for which the equation $Ax = \mathbf{u}$ has a solution.

Problems on Least Squares

1. Let $A = [a_{ij}]$ be the 7×5 matrix defined by $a_{ij} = 1/(i + j)$. Let $\mathbf{v} = (v_i)$ be the 7-vector defined by $v_i = i - 1$. Compute the orthogonal projection **u** of **v** onto the column space of A, and use it to find the least-squares solution of the equation $Ax = \mathbf{v}$ by solving the equation $Ax = \mathbf{u}$. Compare your answer with the result returned by leastsqrs(A,v).

2. Let $A = [a_{ij}]$ be the 5×7 matrix defined by $a_{ij} = \min(i,j)$. Let $\mathbf{v} = (v_i)$ be the 5-vector defined by $v_i = i$. Find the least-squares solution of the equation $Ax = \mathbf{v}$, and use it to compute the orthogonal projection **u** of **v** onto the column space of A.

---

[9]See, for example, Gilbert Strang, *Linear Algebra and Its Applications*, 3rd ed. (New York: Academic Press, 1988).

3. Let $A = [a_{ij}]$ be the 5×5 matrix defined by $a_{ij} = i + j$. Let $\mathbf{v} = (v_i)$ be the 5-vector defined by $v_i = i$.

   a. Find the least-squares solution $\mathbf{u}$ of the equation $A\mathbf{x} = \mathbf{v}$ and use it to find the orthogonal projection $\mathbf{c}$ of $\mathbf{v}$ onto the column space of A.

   b. Find the least-squares solution of the equation $A^T\mathbf{x} = \mathbf{u}$, and use it to compute the orthogonal projection $\mathbf{r}$ of $\mathbf{u}$ onto the row space of A.

   c. Verify that the vector $\mathbf{r}$ of part b is a solution of the equation $A\mathbf{x} = \mathbf{c}$.

   d. Verify that the vector $\mathbf{r}$ of part b is the solution of least norm of the equation $A\mathbf{x} = \mathbf{c}$. (Hint: Any vector $\mathbf{w}$ can be written in one and only one way as the sum $\mathbf{w} = \mathbf{w}_1 + \mathbf{w}_2$, with $\mathbf{w}_1$ in the row space of A and $\mathbf{w}_2$ orthogonal to the row space of A. Consider the inequality $\|\mathbf{w}_1\| + \|\mathbf{w}_2\| \le \|\mathbf{w}_1\| + \|\mathbf{w}_2\|$.)

4. Let $A = [a_{ij}]$ be an $m \times n$ matrix of rank n, so that the columns of A are linearly independent. Then A^tA is an invertible $n \times n$ matrix (verify this). If $\mathbf{w}$ is the orthogonal projection of a vector $\mathbf{b}$ onto the column space C of A, then $\mathbf{w}$ is a linear combination of the columns of A, say $\mathbf{w} = A\mathbf{x}_0$. Hence, $\mathbf{x}_0$ is a least-squares solution of the equation $A\mathbf{x} = \mathbf{b}$, and $\mathbf{b} - A\mathbf{x}_0$ is orthogonal to each of the columns of A. Because the columns of A are the rows of A^t, it follows that $A^t(\mathbf{v} - A\mathbf{x}_0) = \mathbf{0}$, and hence that $A^t\mathbf{v} = A^tA\mathbf{x}_0$. As A^tA is invertible, you can find $\mathbf{x}_0$ by multiplying by A^{-1}; thus, in this case, the least-squares solution $\mathbf{x}_0$ of the equation $A\mathbf{x} = \mathbf{v}$ is given by $\mathbf{x}_0 = (A^tA)^{-1}A^t\mathbf{b}$. Use this formula to find the least-squares solution of the equation $A\mathbf{x} = \mathbf{b}$, where $A = [a_{ij}]$ is the 5×4 matrix with $a_{ij} = \min(i,j)$, $1 \le i \le 5$, $1 \le j \le 4$, and $\mathbf{b} = [b_i]$, with $b_i = i^2$, $1 \le i \le 5$. Compare your solution to the answer returned by `leastsqrs`.

Curve Fitting with Too Many Points
[product]

In Chapter 1, polynomials were fit exactly to data—a polynomial of degree n (or less) to $n + 1$ data points. If you have more than $n + 1$ points through which the graph of a polynomial of degree n must fit, it may not be possible to do the job exactly, but it is possible to obtain a least-squares approximation.

Assume that you have obtained the twenty data points $\mathbf{P}_i(x_i, y_i) = \left(\dfrac{2\pi i}{20}, \sin\left(\dfrac{2\pi i}{20}\right) \right)$, $i = 1, \ldots, 20$, and that you need to fit a polynomial of degree three or less to them. This requires that you determine the vector $\mathbf{a} = (a_1, a_2, a_3, a_4)$ of coefficients for which the 20-vector $\mathbf{w} = (w_i)$ defined by $w_i = \sum\limits_{j=1}^{4} a_j x_i^{j-1}$, $i = 1, \ldots, 20$, is as close as possible to the vector $\mathbf{y} = (y_1, \ldots, y_{20})$. If you form the 20×4 matrix $M = (x_i^{j-1})$, then the problem is to find the least-squares solution $\mathbf{a}$ of the equation $M\mathbf{x} = \mathbf{y}$.

This defines the vector **x** *of x-coordinates.*	• x:=vector(20,i->2*Pi*i/20);
This defines the vector **y** *of y-coordinates and the* 20×4 *matrix* $M = (x_i^{j-1})$.	• y:=vector(20,i->sin(x[i])); • M:=matrix(20,4,(i,j)->x[i]^(j-1));
This assigns **a** *the value of the least-squares solution.*	• a:=leastsqrs(M,y);
You can now define the polynomial p that best fits the data.	• i:='i'; • p:=sum(a[i+1]*t^i,i=0..3);

If t has a value, it will have to be unassigned before this will work as desired.

In situations involving approximations, as this one does, it is interesting to see just how well the approximate answer works. In this case, you can either compare the values $p(x_i)$ with y_i, or plot the points (x_i, y_i) and the graph of $y = p(x)$ together.

This plots all the points (x_i, y_i) *and the graph of* $y = p(x)$ *on the interval* $[0, 2\pi]$.	• plot({seq([x[i],y[i]], » i=1..20),p},x=0..2*Pi);

Note that it is possible that a polynomial of degree three or less—or even the zero polynomial—might better fit the data in some cases. For example, if all the points happened to lie in a line, the coefficients a_2 and a_3 would both turn out to be zero.

Problems on Curve Fitting

1. Let $x_i = \dfrac{2\pi i}{20}$ and $y_i = \sin(x_i)$, $i = 1...20$. Find the polynomial of degree five or less that best fits the data. Compare the result with that obtained in the text example for polynomials of degree three or less.

2. Fitting a polynomial by least squares gives the best possible answer, but it need not always be close. For example, let $q = \displaystyle\prod_{i=1}^{5} i(x - 3)$. You can enter q with *Maple*'s product command—which has the same form as the sum and seq commands—and use expand to put it into standard form. Generate ten data points (x_i, y_i) from the graph of q, using $x = 1, 2, ..., 10$ and compute the polynomial p of degree three or less that gives the best least-squares fit. Plot the points (x_i, y_i) together with p, and note

that the shape of p is a good fit to the points. Now, compute the minimum difference $y_i - p(x_i)$. (You can partially automate this by applying *Maple*'s min function to the sequence of differences.)

Curve Fitting with Other Inner Products

When working with functions, it makes good sense to measure the distance between two functions by using the integral. You can do this by defining the inner product $\langle f,g \rangle$ of functions f and g to be the integral $\int_a^b f(x)g(x)dx$ on some predetermined interval $[a,b]$. The associated norm is given by $\|f - g\|^2 = \int_{x=a}^b (f(x) - g(x))^2 dx$, which is roughly related to the area between the graphs.

Assume, for example, that you want to find the polynomial expression of degree five or less whose graph best fits the graph of $\sin(x)$ on the interval $[0,2\pi]$. This has practical applications, because polynomials are much easier to evaluate than transcendental functions such as sine. You proceed as with the Euclidean inner product; the problem is to project $\sin(x)$ orthogonally onto the space $\mathbf{P}_5$ of all polynomials of degree five or less.

This defines the inner product.

```
• iprod:=proc(f,g)
»   int(f*g,x=0..2*Pi)
» end;
```

This is $\int_0^{2\pi} f(x)g(x)dx$.

Define the projection of a function f onto a function g.

```
• proj:=proc(f,g)
»   (iprod(f,g)/iprod(g,g))*g
» end;
```
The parentheses grouping iprod(f,g)/iprod(g,g) are not necessary because of *Maple*'s evaluation rules.

This defines the standard basis for $\mathbf{P}_5$.

```
• for i from 1 to 6
» do
»     v[i]:=x^(i-1)
» od;
```

With the exception of the bound on i, this uses the same code that was used in Section 2.6 to apply Gram-Schmidt with the Euclidean inner product.

```
• j:='j';
• for i to 6
» do
»    w[i]:=v[i]-sum('proj(v[i],w[j])',
»     j=1..i-1)
» od;
```
The quotes around the `proj()` term are required to force the evaluation in the desired order.

You can now compute the orthogonal projection psin *of* sin(x) *onto* **P**$_5$.

```
• i:='i';
• psin:=
» sum('proj(sin(x),w[i])',
» i=1..6);
```
Again, the quotes around the `proj()` term are required to force the evaluation in the desired order.

You may find it of interest to plot sin(x) *and* psin *together. Note that* psin *is an expression, so you do not use* psin(x) *in the plot statement.*

```
• plot({psin,sin(x)},
» x=0..2*Pi);
```
Note that it appears that there is only one curve in the plot—the fit is very good.

Additional Problems on Curve Fitting

1. Find the polynomial of degree seven or less that best approximates cosine on the interval $[0,\pi]$.

2. The polynomials obtained from the Gram-Schmidt procedure from the standard basis 1, x, x^2, ... with the inner product $\langle f,g \rangle = \int_{-1}^{1} f(x)g(x)dx$

   are called the Legendre polynomials. In particular, the nth term is called the nth Legendre polynomial. The Legendre polynomials are contained in the *Maple* package `orthopoly`. They are accessible only after loading the `orthopoly` package using the command `with(orthopoly)`. Once loaded, the package assigns procedure values to the variables G, L, U, H, P, and T. The nth Legendre polynomial is then given by $P(n,x)$.

   Use the P function to generate the first seven Legendre polynomials and to find the polynomial p in **P**$_6$ that best approximates the function $f(x) = \sin(x) + \cos(x)$ on the interval $[-1,1]$, relative to the given inner product.

3 Eigenspaces

Eigenvalues and eigenvectors (also known as characteristic values and characteristic vectors) are frequently applied topics commonly studied in undergraduate mathematics. Recall that λ is an eigenvalue and $\mathbf{v} \neq \mathbf{0}$ is an associated eigenvector for A if $A\mathbf{v} = \lambda\mathbf{v}$. If, for example, multiplication by A represents the action of some force or forces on a physical system with components represented by the vector $\mathbf{v}$, and if $A\mathbf{v} = \lambda\mathbf{v}$, then the components of the system are all changing at the same rate. If $\lambda = 1$, then the system is static.

3.1 Eigenvalues and Eigenvectors
```
[ allvalues, charmat, charpoly, companion,
eigenvects, evalc, evalf, factor, op, RootOf, solve ]
```

Within the limits imposed by the time and resources available to it, *Maple* is capable of describing the eigenvalues and eigenvectors of any rational matrix. (Although *Maple* is not strictly limited to matrices with rational entries, we will use only rational examples. Use `?eigenvects` for more information.)

You should begin your session as usual.
```
• with(linalg):
• alias(Id=&*());
```

Here is a 4 × 4 matrix A that is fairly typical of those commonly used to study eigenvalue/eigenvector problems.
```
• f:=proc(i,j)
» if i=j then i+j-1 else i+j+1 fi end;

• A:=matrix(4,4,f);
```

You can compute the characteristic matrix xI – A and characteristic polynomial |xI – A| from the definitions.

- `evalm(x*Id - A);`
- `p:=det(");`[1]

This is one of the most important applications of the determinant.

You can use `solve` *to find the eigenvalues.*

- `lambda:=solve(p=0,x);`

The eigenvalues are the terms of the sequence that is returned.

The λ_i-eigenspace is the null space of the matrix $\lambda_i I - A$. Because two of the eigenvalues are not rational, the procedure used in Chapter 2 for finding the null space will not work here—`rref`, `gausselim`, and so on will accept only matrices with rational entries. Instead, you can use *Maple*'s built-in `nullspace` command, which returns a basis for the null space of a matrix.

The λ_i-eigenspace is the nullspace of the matrix $\lambda_i I - A$.

- `nullspace(lambda[1]*Id - A);`

The set that is returned is a basis for the λ_1-eigenspace. You may wish to repeat the process for the other two eigenvalues.

One special property of the matrix A is that its characteristic polynomial has no factors of degree greater than two.

- `factor(p);`

The `factor` command returns a factorization of the form $rp_1{}^{e_1}p_2{}^{e_2} \ldots p_k{}^{e_k}$, where r is a rational number and each p_i is a polynomial with integer coefficients.

The approach demonstrated for A will work for any rational matrix, as long as none of the factors p_i of the characteristic polynomial has degree three or greater. In general, however, characteristic polynomials can have factors of any degree.

Here, B is an example of a matrix with a characteristic polynomial with irreducible factors of degree three and four.[2]

- `p:=expand((x^3-x+1)*(x^4-20*x^2+10));`
- `B:=companion(p,x);`
- `p:=factor(det(x*Id - B));`

The matrix B is called the *companion matrix* of the polynomial p; it arises because p is its characteristic polynomial. You may want to see if you can prove this in general.

---

[1]*Maple* also has the built-in commands `charmat` and `charpoly` that can be used to compute the characteristic matrix and characteristic polynomial.

[2]Throughout, *irreducible* is used to mean irreducible over the rational numbers.

In this case, the descriptions of the eigenvalues by radicals are fairly complicated for the equation $(\lambda I - B)\mathbf{x} = 0$ to be solved by nullspace.[3]

- `lambda:=solve(p=0,x);`
- `for i to 6`
- » `do`
- » `nullspace(lambda[i]*Id-B)`
- » `od;`

In the initial release of *Maple V*, nullspace fails here. Code for a later release took more than twenty minutes to run in a test.

The description by radicals of a root of a cubic or quartic factor is quite complex; this constitutes a barrier that complicates the computation of the eigenvectors of matrices larger than 2 × 2. (All symbolic computation programs suffer from this difficulty.) Even more troublesome is the fact that there are no analogues of the quadratic, cubic, and quartic formulas for polynomials of degree five or greater. To break through these barriers, *Maple* provides a simpler representation of the roots of the characteristic polynomial that will function with nullspace: If p is a polynomial in x, then RootOf(p) is a parameter that can stand for any of the roots of the polynomial p.[4] We will favor the RootOf representation over the radical representation of roots in calculations throughout the sequel: It is more reliable and more efficient.

The RootOf *function is typically applied to the factors of the characteristic polynomial.*

- `facts:=op(factor(p));`
- `p1:=facts[1];`
- `lambda:='lambda';`
- `lambda[1]:=RootOf(p1);`

When applied to a product, the op command returns the sequence of factors—facts[1] is the first term in the sequence. The factorization returned by factor has the form $rp_1{}^{e_1}p_2{}^{e_2} \ldots p_k{}^{e_k}$. If $r = 1$, then *Maple* simplifies the expression so that $p_1{}^{e_1}$ is the first factor. However, if $r \neq 1$, then `facts[1] = r`.

By the Fundamental Theorem of Algebra, a factor p_i of degree d will have exactly d distinct (though possibly complex) roots, and no two distinct factors p_i and p_j will have a common root.

Use nullspace *to obtain a basis of the eigenspace.*

- `NS:=nullspace(lambda[1]*Id - B);`

It takes a little practice to read the style of output that results.

You can simplify the notation considerably by aliasing a name to the RootOf.

- `alias(t=lambda[1]);`
- `NS;`

In this context, t is a parameter that can stand for any of the three roots of p_1. It is important to keep in mind that the apparently single basis that is

---

[3]Although the nullspace command is enhanced to handle such equations in later releases, it fails in the first release of *Maple V*.

[4]RootOf(p,x) is an example of an algebraic number.

returned actually represents three different bases—one for each of the three roots of p_1.

You can use `allvalues` *to convert a* `RootOf` *into radical form when possible.*

- `all:=allvalues(t);`

The translation to radical form can always be accomplished if the polynomial has degree four or less. However, there is in general no description by radicals of the roots of a polynomial of degree five or greater.

When `allvalues` cannot find a description by radicals, it will attempt to find decimal approximations of the exact answers.

If you wish, you can substitute the radical forms for the parameters in the basis vector(s).

- `ES[1]:=subs(t=all[1],evalm(NS));`

Similar statements substituting `t=all[2]`, ... into NS give the bases for the eigenspaces associated with the other roots of p_1. (Note that p_1 could be either factor here. The factors will not necessarily be returned in the same order from session to session.)

Old aliases (like other potential troublemakers) should be eliminated.

- `alias(t=t);`

A few properties of `RootOf` *worth noting are illustrated here.*

- `RootOf(2*x - 3/2);`
- `RootOf((x^2 - 1)^2);`
- `RootOf(3,x);`

Some simplification of `RootOf` expressions may be done automatically, but trying to apply `RootOf` to a constant results in an error message.

If you want all the eigenvalues of a matrix in `RootOf` *form, you can* `map` `RootOf` *onto the set of factors.*

- `factor(det(x*Id - A));`
- `op(");`
- `map(RootOf,{"});`

When applied to a product, the `op` command returns the sequence of factors. Recall that `map` is used to apply a function or operation to the entries of a data structure—in this case, a set.

Frequently, it is important to know whether the eigenvalues of a matrix are rational, real, or complex.

If the eigenvalues are in radical form, Maple's complex number evaluator, `evalc`, *will attempt to write them in the form* $a + bi$ *with a and b real.*

- `allc:=evalc({all});`

Recall that the variable `all` was previously assigned the value returned by `allvalues(lambda[1])`.

If applied to a set, `evalc` is automatically mapped onto the elements of the set. This is true for lists as well, but not for sequences or arrays.

In Release 2, simplification of complex numbers to the form $a + bi$ is automatic.

*If you want more informa-
tion on the eigenvalues, you
can also apply the* evalf
command.

- evalf(");

There is always the possibility that rounding errors may mislead you in some cases.

If applied to a set, evalf (like evalc) is automatically mapped onto the elements of the set.

You might try using the evalf and evalc functions in the opposite order to see a small effect of rounding errors.

For factors of degree five or greater, floating-point approximation and graphing are the only tools available other than RootOf.

EXERCISES 3.1 _____

1. Find all the eigenvalues and eigenvectors of the 9×9 matrix $A = [a_{ij}]$ with $a_{ij} = 1$ for all i and j.

2. Find all the eigenvalues and eigenvectors of the companion matrix of the polynomial

$$p = 1 - x + x^2 - x^3 + x^4$$

Determine which of the eigenvalues are real and which are complex.

3. Find the eigenvalues and eigenvectors of the 4×4 matrix $B = [b_{ij}]$, where, for each i and j, b_{ij} is the minimum of i and j. Determine which of the eigenvalues are real and which are complex.

4. Find the eigenvalues and eigenvectors of the 3×3 matrix $Q = [q_{ij}]$, where, for each i and j, $q_{ij} = \dfrac{i}{j}$. Determine which of the eigenvalues are real and which are complex.

3.2 Similarity

Eigenvalues and eigenvectors have a broad spectrum of applications. This is due in large part to the role they play in *similarity theory*. Two square matrices A and B are said to be *similar* if B satisfies an equation of the form $B = P^{-1}AP$. The collection of all matrices similar to a given matrix A is called the similarity class of A.

It is often possible to simplify the solution of a matrix (or matrix/ vector) equation by substitution of a similar matrix for the original. For example: Given a matrix equation $Y = AX$ and a matrix $B = P^{-1}AP$, substituting $X = P\overline{X} =$ and $Y = P\overline{Y}$ into the equation, and then left-multiplying by P^{-1} yields the equivalent equation $P^{-1}P\overline{Y} = P^{-1}AP\overline{X}$, which simplifies to $\overline{Y} = B\overline{X}$. If B has a particularly simple form, the new equation may be much easier to solve than the original. If so, X and Y are easily obtained from $\overline{X}$ and $\overline{Y}$. In practice, substitution using similar matrices is particularly important when X and Y are known only through the equation $Y = AX$ and an additional relation, as when $X = [x_i(t)]$ is a column of functions and Y is the column of derivatives $[x_i'(t)]$. In matrix notation this is written $X' = AX$.

The simplest representative one might hope to find of the similarity class of a matrix A would be a scalar matrix λI; however, the similarity class of λI consists only of λI itself. Hence, for nonscalar matrices, the simplest representative one might hope to find would be a "block scalar" matrix— a diagonal matrix. A matrix A that is similar to a diagonal matrix Dg is said to be diagonalizable; the process of finding a diagonal matrix Dg similar to A is called diagonalization of A.

Recall that an $n \times n$ matrix A is diagonalizable if and only if it has n linearly independent eigenvectors. This, in turn, is equivalent to the condition that for each eigenvalue λ of A, the dimension of the null space of $\lambda I - A$ is equal to the multiplicity of λ as a root of the characteristic polynomial $C_A(x) = \det(xI - A)$ of A.

3.2.1 Similarity and Diagonalization
`[ diag, jordan ]`

The restriction to rational matrices remains in effect.

The matrix A is a good first example.

- `f:=proc(i,j)`
- » `  if i=j then 0 else 1 fi`
- » `end;`

- `A:=matrix(7,7,f);`

The matrix A is symmetric, and symmetric matrices are always diagonalizable.

- `p:=det(x*Id - A);`
- `op(factor(p));`
- `lambda:=map(RootOf,{"});`

A has only the two eigenvalues -1 and 6.

You can use the bases of the eigenspaces to form a diagonalizing matrix.

- `ES[1]:=nullspace(lambda[1]*Id-A);`
- `ES[2]:=nullspace(lambda[2]*Id-A);`

In each case, the number of basis vectors is the same as the multiplicity of λ_i as a root of p. Notice that the results are sets.

Use op *and* augment *to construct the diagonalizing matrix.*

- `P:=augment(op(ES[1]),op(ES[2]));`

The op function returns the contents of the sets as sequences. Two sequences separated by a comma form a sequence, so this command applies augment to the sequence of eigenvectors in the bases.

Maple can verify that $P^{-1}AP$ is diagonal.

- `evalm(1/P &* A &* P);`

The eigenvalues appear on the diagonal according to the ordering of the vectors in P. You might wish to compare this result with that obtained when the roles of $ES[1]$ and $ES[2]$ are reversed in the definition of P.

In some cases, the descriptions of the eigenvalues and eigenvectors are more complicated.

The matrix B defined here will present an obstacle not encountered in diagonalizing A.

- `g:=proc(i,j)`
» `  if i=j then i+j-1 else i+j fi`
» `end;`

- `B:=matrix(5,5,g);`

Find the eigenvalues.

- `p:=det(x*Id - B);`
- `factor(p);`
- `lambda:=map(RootOf,{op(")});`

The eigenvalues can appear in either order in the set. In our session, -1 is first; the second eigenvalue, λ_2, is more complex.

At this point, you cannot be sure that B is diagonalizable. In this case, there are just three distinct eigenvalues. Since the `RootOf` involved is of degree two, an explicit description of the eigenvalues can be obtained in terms of radicals.

It is helpful to alias any remaining `RootOf`.

- `alias(t=lambda[2]);`

In our case, λ_2 is a `RootOf`. If λ_2 is not the `RootOf` in your session as well, you will have to make appropriate changes.

Find the eigenspace bases.

- `ES[1]:=nullspace(lambda[1]*Id - B);`
- `ES[2..3]:=nullspace(lambda[2]*Id - B);`

Note that *ES*[2..3] actually represents two eigenspace bases, not just one—hence the notation.

You can convert the `RootOf` *to radical form for the purpose of describing the diagonalizing matrix.*

- `all:=allvalues(t);`

The conversion is not possible in some cases, but it is possible (and probably desirable) in this case.

You can obtain the other two eigenspace bases simply by using `subs`.

- `ES[2]:=subs(t=all[1],ES[2..3]);`
- `ES[3]:=subs(t=all[2],ES[2..3]);`

Note that, because the vectors are in a set, `subs` works without `evalm`.

You can now build the diagonalizing matrix in the same manner you used earlier for A.

- `Q:=augment(op(ES[1]),op(ES[2]),op(ES[3]));`

Because each *ES[i]* is a set, it is necessary to extract the operands (elements) for `augment`.

For matrices with several eigenspaces, you may want to use the `seq` *function to save some typing.*

- `augment(seq(op(ES[i]),i=1..3));`

Note that this is shorter than the style just used to define *Q*.

Dispose of the alias t.	• `alias(t=t);`

Here is an example with a quintic characteristic polynomial that is irreducible.

Define the indicated 5×5 *matrix.*	• `C:=matrix(5,5,max);`

It appears that all matrices defined with the `max` function may have characteristic polynomials that are irreducible.

Calculate the characteristic polynomial and get the eigenvalues.	• `p:=det(x*Id - C);` • `factor(p);` • `lambda:={RootOf(")};`

In this case, you don't use `op`, as there is only one factor. Also, there is no need to use `map`.

Alias t *to the* RootOf.	• `alias(t=lambda[1]);`

Compute the eigenspace bases.	• `ES[1..5]:=nullspace(lambda[1]*Id - C);`

In this case, there are no rational eigenvalues. However, there are five distinct eigenvalues, so *C* is diagonalizable. In fact, because *C* is symmetric, it is an important theorem of linear algebra that its eigenvalues are all real.[5]

Use allvalues.	• `all:=allvalues(t);`

In this case, `allvalues` only gives approximations of the five eigenvalues.

You can create an accurate formal description of the bases of the eigenspaces simply by substituting unassigned variable names for the RootOf.	• `for i to 5 do` » `ES[i]:=subs(t=r[i],ES[1..5]) od;`

The formal descriptions of the basis vectors can be used to give a description of a diagonalizing matrix.

This gives a symbolic description of a diagonalizing matrix P_s *and the diagonalized matrix* D_s. *Note the use of the* diag *command.*	• `Ps:=augment(seq(op(ES[i]),i=1..5));` • `Ds:=diag(seq(r[i],i=1..5));`

These are meaningful descriptions, with the addendum that r_1, r_2, ..., r_5 are the roots of the polynomial

$$p = x^5 - 15x^4 - 85x^3 - 98x^2 - 39x - 5.$$

[5]For more information, see any standard text on linear algebra (for example, Strang, *Linear Algebra and Its Applications,* 3rd ed., New York: Academic Press, 1988).

You can use the values from all *to get a floating-point approximation of the eigenvectors, the diagonalizing matrix P, and the diagonalized matrix D.*

- ```
  for i to 5
  ```
» ```
  do ESf[i]:=subs(t=all[i],ES[1..5]) od;
  ```

- ```
  Pf:=augment(seq(op(ESf[i]),i=1..5));
  ```

- ```
  Df:=diag(seq(all[i],i=1..5));
  ```
The approximations of the eigenvalues should be fairly good.

You may find it interesting to compare D_f with $P_f^{-1}CP_f$.

- ```
  evalm(1/Pf &* C &*Pf);
  ```
Note the rounding errors.

Unassign the alias for t.

- ```
  alias(t=t);
  ```

Here is an example with complex eigenvalues.

Note that the matrix M is not symmetric.

- ```
  i:='i';
  ```
- ```
  p:=sum(x^i,i=1..4);
  ```
- ```
  M:=companion(p,x);
  ```

Find the eigenvalues.

- ```
  factor(det(x*Id-M));
  ```
- ```
  lambda:=map(RootOf,{op(")});
  ```
RootOf($\_Z^2$ +1) is a familiar number (or pair of numbers).

Alias t *to the* RootOf.

- ```
  alias(t=lambda[3]);
  ```
This assumes *Maple* returned the RootOf in the third position. If not, you will have to adjust the command appropriately.

Compute the eigenspace bases.

- ```
  ES[1]:=nullspace(lambda[1]*Id - M);
  ```
- ```
  ES[2]:=nullspace(lambda[2]*Id - M);
  ```
- ```
  ES[3..4]:=nullspace(lambda[3]*Id - M);
  ```

Compute the radical forms of the roots of t.

- ```
  all:=allvalues(t);
  ```
If you still have *I* aliased to $\sqrt{-1}$, be sure to distinguish between *I* and 1. The values of all are **i** and **–i**.

Find bases for the eigenspaces of the values of t.

- ```
  ES[3]:=subs(t=all[1],ES[3..4]);
  ```
- ```
  ES[4]:=subs(t=all[2],ES[3..4]);
  ```

You may find this makes it easier to form the diagonalized matrix.

- ```
  eigvals:=map(allvalues,lambda);
  ```
  ```

Form the diagonalized matrix and an associated transition matrix.

- `Dg:=diag(op(eigvals));`

- `P:=augment(seq(op(ES[i]),i=1..4));`

Unalias t.

- `alias(t=t);` .

Diagonalizing with `jordan`

In addition to the techniques thus far discussed, you can also use *Maple*'s `jordan` command to diagonalize matrices. If *Maple* can compute the eigenvalues exactly (without using `RootOf`), they will appear on the main diagonal of the result returned by `jordan`; otherwise, the entries on the main diagonal of the result will be decimal approximations of the eigenvalues. If `jordan` is applied to a matrix that is not diagonalizable, the result is an upper-triangular matrix.

The `jordan` command has the highly useful additional property that it can be applied using a second argument that is assigned a matrix value and that acts as a transition matrix. For example, the command `J:=jordan(A,Q)` returns an upper-triangular matrix *J*—using exact values if the eigenvalues can be so calculated (without using `RootOf`), and approximate numbers otherwise—and assigns *Q* a value such that $QAQ^{-1} = J$. As previously noted, the matrix *J* is diagonal if *A* is diagonalizable.

Because we compute a transition matrix *P* so that $P^{-1}AP = J$, we will often use `jordan(A,Q)` and define $P = Q^{-1}$. Nevertheless, the `jordan` command frequently provides an easy way to find an invertible matrix *P* and a diagonal or upper-triangular matrix $J = P^{-1}AP$.

The matrix *J* returned by the `jordan` command is always block-diagonal. The diagonal blocks have ones or zeros on the first superdiagonal, a constant diagonal value (which is an eigenvalue of *A*), and zeros elsewhere. The diagonal blocks are called *simple Jordan blocks*. For example, the 3×3 matrix

$$\begin{bmatrix} \lambda & 1 & 0 \\ 0 & \lambda & 1 \\ 0 & 0 & \lambda \end{bmatrix}$$

is a simple Jordan block. Though some authors put the ones on the main subdiagonal, *Maple* puts them on the main superdiagonal.

Consider again the example $M = \begin{bmatrix} 0 & 0 & 0 & 0 \\ 1 & 0 & 0 & -1 \\ 0 & 1 & 0 & -1 \\ 0 & 0 & 0 & -1 \end{bmatrix}$.

Use jordan *to get both the diagonalized form of M and a transition matrix.*

- J:=jordan(M,Q);
- P:=inverse(Q);

Check the result.

- evalm(1/P &* M &* P);

The matrix *P* may well differ from that obtained above.

As the preceding example shows, jordan can save a significant amount of time. Unfortunately, its implementation in the initial release of *Maple V* is imperfect.

In the initial release of Maple V, jordan *fails occasionally.*

- jordan(matrix(3,3,1));

A patch to jordan is possible if it fails here.[6]

Exercises on Diagonalization

In each of the following exercises, determine whether the matrix as defined is diagonalizable; if so, find a diagonalizing matrix *P*.

1. The 5×5 matrix $A = [a_{ij}]$, with $a_{ij} = \begin{cases} i + j - 1 \text{ if } i = j \\ i + j + 1 \text{ if } i \neq j \end{cases}$.

2. The 4×4 matrix $B = [b_{ij}]$, with $b_{ij} = \begin{cases} 1 \text{ if } i > j \\ 0 \text{ otherwise} \end{cases}$.

3. The 5×5 matrix $C = [c_{ij}]$, with $c_{ij} = \begin{cases} 2 \text{ if } i = j \\ 1 \text{ if } i \neq j \end{cases}$.

4. The 4×4 matrix $H = [h_{ij}]$, defined by $h_{ij} = 1/(i + j - 1)$. (*H* is the 4×4 *Hilbert matrix*.)

5. The 4×4 matrix $M = [m_{ij}]$, defined by $m_{ij} = \min(i,j)$.

3.2.2 Similarity and Triangularization

It may not be possible to diagonalize a given square matrix *A*; however, if a factorization $C_A(x) = \prod_{i=1}^{n} (x - \lambda_i)$ of the characteristic polynomial can be found, then it is always possible to find an upper-triangular matrix $T = [t_{ij}]$ (with $t_{ii} = \lambda_i$) that is similar to *A*. Note that if $P^{-1}AP = T$, then substituting

---

[6]The patch for the jordan command is accomplished by changing one line in each of the two procedures " `linalg/jordan/makeJ` " and " `linalg/jordan/makeQJ` ". In each case, the line "elif type(q,`^`) or type(q,`+`) then …" must have the additional option "or type (q,name)" added. You can make this change yourself. For example, to fix " `linalg/jordan/makeJ` ", give the commands interface(verboseproc=2) and print(`linalg/jordan/makeJ`). Depending on the machine you are working on, you will either be able to edit the output or have to redefine the procedure. In the latter case, the easiest fix is to alter the line indicated by changing type(q,`+`) to type(q,{`+`,name}).

$Y = P\overline{Y}$ and $X = P\overline{X}$ into the equation $Y = AX$, and left-multiplying by P^{-1}, yields the equivalent upper-triangular system $\overline{Y} = T\overline{X}$. Often, in applications, this equivalent system can be solved using back-substitution.

There is a technique for triangularizing an $n \times n$ matrix A, based on the following four observations.

1. If $\lambda_1, \lambda_2, \ldots, \lambda_s$ are eigenvalues of A with associated linearly independent eigenvectors $\mathbf{v}_1, \mathbf{v}_2, \ldots, \mathbf{v}_s$, respectively; and if $\mathbf{v}_1, \mathbf{v}_2, \ldots, \mathbf{v}_n$ is a basis for $\Re^n$; then the matrix $P_1 = [\mathbf{v}_1, \mathbf{v}_2, \ldots, \mathbf{v}_n]$ satisfies

$$P_1^{-1}AP_1 = \begin{bmatrix} \lambda_1 & * & \cdots & * & * \\ 0 & \lambda_2 & & * & * \\ & & \cdots & & \\ 0 & 0 & \cdots & \lambda_s & * \\ 0 & 0 & \cdots & 0 & A_{s+1} \end{bmatrix}$$

where A_{s+1} is an $(n-s) \times (n-s)$ matrix.

2. The eigenvalues of A_{s+1} are a subset of the eigenvalues of A.

3. If $P_1^{-1}AP_1$ is defined as in observation 1, and if the matrix Q triangularizes A_{s+1}, then the matrix $P_2 = \text{diag}(1, \ldots, 1, Q)$ triangularizes the matrix $P_1^{-1}AP_1$.

4. If P_2 is defined as in observation 3, then the matrix $P = P_1P_2$ triangularizes A.

The following example demonstrates this technique.

Consider the companion matrix A of $q = x^4 - 2x^2 + 1$.

- `q:=x^4-2*x^2+1;`

- `A:=companion(q,x);`

The matrix A is not diagonalizable.

Find the eigenvalues of the matrix A.

- `p:=det(x*Id - A);`
- `factor(");`
- `op(");`
- `lambda:=map(RootOf,{"});`

A has just the two eigenvalues 1 and −1. (Note that $p = q$.)

Find the eigenspaces.

- `ES[1]:=nullspace(lambda[1]*Id - A);`
- `ES[2]:=nullspace(lambda[2]*Id - A);`

Both eigenspaces are one-dimensional, whereas each λ_i has multiplicity two as a root of p.

Extract the eigenvectors.

- `v[1]:=ES[1][1];`
- `v[2]:=ES[2][1];`

The first and only element of each basis is the desired vector.

Extend the eigenvectors $\mathbf{v}_1$, $\mathbf{v}_2$ to a basis $\mathbf{v}_1$, $\mathbf{v}_2$, $\mathbf{v}_3$, $\mathbf{v}_4$ for $\Re^4$.

- `S:=stack(v[1],v[2]);`
- `N:=nullspace(S);`
- `v[3]:=N[1];`
- `v[4]:=N[2];`

The vectors $\mathbf{v}_1$, $\mathbf{v}_2$, $\mathbf{v}_3$, $\mathbf{v}_4$ form a basis for $\Re^4$. (Can you explain why?)

Set up the matrix $P_1 = [\mathbf{v}_1,\mathbf{v}_2,\mathbf{v}_3,\mathbf{v}_4]$ and use it to partially triangularize A.

- `P1:=augment(seq(v[i],i=1..4));`

- `T1:=evalm(1/P1 &*A &* P1);`

The matrix P_1 partially triangularizes the matrix A, leaving a 2×2 submatrix in the lower right-hand corner to be dealt with.

Extract the untriangularized lower right-hand submatrix.

- `A3:=submatrix(",3..4,3..4);`

Find a triangularizing matrix for A_3.

Find the eigenvalues of the matrix A_3.

- `det(x*Id - A3);`
- `factor(");`
- `lambda:=map(RootOf,{op(")});`

Notice that the eigenvalues of A_3 are eigenvalues of A. Verify the fact that this will always be the case.

Find bases for the eigenspaces of A_3.

- `v[1]:=nullspace(lambda[1]*Id - A3)[1];`
- `v[2]:=nullspace(lambda[2]*Id - A3)[1];`

This "recycles" the names $\mathbf{v}_1$ and $\mathbf{v}_2$ for the eigenvectors of A_3.

Set up the matrices $Q = [\mathbf{v}_1,\mathbf{v}_2]$ *and* $P_2 = \mathrm{diag}(1,1,Q)$.

- `Q:=augment(v[1],v[2]);`
- `P2:=diag(1,1,Q);`

The matrix P_2 is invertible and triangularizes the matrix T_1; can you see why? You may wish to verify this.

The matrix $P = P_1P_2$ now triangularizes A.

- `P:=evalm(P1 &* P2);`
- `evalm(1/P &* A &* P);`

Can you explain why the product $P = P_1P_2$ triangularizes A?

Triangularizing with `jordan`

In Section 3.2.1, you saw several methods for diagonalizing matrices. In particular, you saw that you can use *Maple*'s `jordan` command in many cases. The command `J:=jordan(A,Q)` always returns an upper-triangular matrix *J*—using exact values if the eigenvalues can be so calculated (without using `RootOf`'s), and approximate numbers otherwise—and assigns *Q* a value such that $QAQ^{-1} = J$.

Consider again the matrix

$$A = \begin{bmatrix} 0 & 0 & 0 & -1 \\ 1 & 0 & 0 & 0 \\ 0 & 1 & 0 & 2 \\ 0 & 0 & 1 & 0 \end{bmatrix}$$

Compute the Jordan form of A (the matrix returned by jordan*) and a transition matrix.*

- J:=jordan(A,Q);
- P:=inverse(Q);

If you get the error message "Illegal use of a formal parameter" when you define *J*, re-enter the jordan command with *Q* in single quotes. This message will appear only if *Q* is assigned a value that is not an array or another type of table.

Check that the transition matrix works as it should.

- evalm(1/P &* A &* P);

Exercises on Triangularization

In Exercises 1–4, triangularize the matrices.

1. $A = [a_{ij}]$, where $a_{ij} = \begin{cases} 1 \text{ if } i > j \\ 0 \text{ otherwise} \end{cases}$.

2. $B = [b_{ij}]$, where $b_{ij} = \begin{cases} 1 \text{ if } i + j \text{ is odd} \\ 0 \text{ if } i + j \text{ is even} \end{cases}$.

3. $C = [c_{ij}]$, where $c_{ij} = \begin{cases} 2 \text{ if } i < j \\ 1 \text{ if } i \geq j \end{cases}$.

4. $F = [f_{ij}]$, where $f_{ij} = \begin{cases} 0 \text{ if } i = j \\ 1 \text{ if } i \neq j \end{cases}$.

3.2.3   Orthogonal Diagonalization

Assume that *A* is a square real matrix and that all the eigenvalues of *A* are real. Shur's Theorem says that *A* is similar to an upper-triangular matrix, and that the triangularizing matrix *P* can be chosen so that $P^T = P^{-1}$, that is, so that *P* is orthogonal.[7] If *A* is symmetric, *P* is orthogonal, and $P^{-1}AP = U$ is upper-triangular, then the relation $P^{-1} = P^T$ yields $U^T = (P^TAP)^T = P^TAP = U$.

Unfortunately, the transition matrix obtained from jordan is usually not orthogonal. However, an orthogonal diagonalizing matrix *N* can be

[7]Charles G. Cullen, *Linear Algebra and Differential Equations* (Boston: Prindle, Weber & Schmidt, 1979).

computed from any diagonalizing matrix P by using the Gram-Schmidt procedure with normalization, on the columns of P. For example, consider the matrix

$$A = \begin{bmatrix} 1 & 4 & 5 \\ 4 & 3 & 6 \\ 5 & 6 & 5 \end{bmatrix}$$

A is symmetric, and therefore orthogonally diagonalizable. (It is also true that a real matrix is orthogonally diagonalizable *only* if it is symmetric; can you prove this?)

This defines the matrix A using a generating function f.

- `f:=proc(i,j)`
- » `if i=j then i+j-1 else i+j+1 fi end;`

- `A:=matrix(3,3,f);`

Apply `jordan` *to A.*

- `J:=jordan(A,Q);`
- `P:=inverse(Q);`

Use Gram-Schmidt with normalization on the columns of P.

- `S:=seq(col(P,i),i=1..3);`
- `G[1]:=S[1];`
- `G[2]:=evalm(S[2]-`
- » `innerprod(S[2],G[1])/innerprod(G[1],G[1])*G[1]);`
- `G[3]:=evalm(S[3]-`
- » `innerprod(S[3],G[1])/innerprod(G[1],G[1])*G[1]`
- » `- innerprod(S[3],G[2])/innerprod(G[2],G[2])*G[2]);`
- `seq(G[i]/norm(G[i],2),i=1..3);`

Recall that the Euclidean norm of a vector **v** is given by `norm(v,2)`.

Form the orthonormal basis vectors into a matrix (as columns).

- `N:=augment(");`

The matrix N will orthogonally diagonalize A.

Check the result.

- `evalm(transpose(N) &* A &* N);`

Exercises on Orthogonal Diagonalization

1. Prove that an orthogonally diagonalizable real matrix is symmetric.
2. Orthogonally diagonalize the 5×5 matrix $A = [a_{ij}]$ defined by $a_{ij} = 1$, $i,j = 1...5$.
3. Orthogonally diagonalize the 6×6 matrix $B = [b_{ij}]$ defined by

$$b_{ij} = \begin{cases} 1 & \text{if } i + j \text{ is even} \\ 0 & \text{if } i + j \text{ is odd} \end{cases}$$

4. Orthogonally diagonalize the matrix $C = [c_{ij}]$ defined by

$$c_{ij} = \begin{cases} 1 \text{ if } i \neq j \\ 0 \text{ otherwise} \end{cases}$$

3.2.4   Similarity, Smith Form, and Frobenius Form
[smith, frobenius]

Smith Form

One very interesting and useful similarity theorem is that two $n \times n$ matrices A and B are similar if and only if their characteristic matrices $M_A(x) = xI - A$ and $M_B(x) = xI - B$ are *equivalent*—that is, if and only if $M_B(x)$ can be obtained from $M_A(x)$ by a sequence of elementary row and column operations. (The elementary operations `mulrow` and `mulcol` are restricted to multiplication by scalars to make the operations reversible; this restriction is not necessary for `addrow` and `addcol`.)

Every matrix $M(x)$ with polynomial entries can be transformed by a sequence of elementary row and column operations into an equivalent diagonal matrix $S = \text{diag}(p_1, p_2, \ldots, p_k, 0, \ldots, 0)$ where, for each $i = 1\ldots k$, p_i is a monic factor of p_{i+1}. The matrix S is uniquely determined by $M(x)$ and is called the *Smith form* of $M(x)$. Two matrices with polynomial entries are equivalent if and only if they have the same Smith form.

A logical consequence of the theorem just stated is that two numerical matrices A and B are similar if and only if their characteristic matrices $xI - A$ and $xI - B$ have the same Smith form. The nonconstant polynomials on the diagonal of the Smith form of A are called the *invariant factors* of A.

Maple can compute the Smith form of any matrix with polynomial entries.

- `M:=matrix(3,3, (i,j)->x^i-j );`
- `smith(M,x);`

Frobenius Form

It follows from the preceding discussion that the polynomials on the diagonal of the Smith form of the matrix $xI - A$ determine which matrices are similar to A. Not surprisingly, the companion matrices of these polynomials also determine the similarity class of A. The block-diagonal matrix F, with the companion matrices of these nonconstant polynomials as diagonal blocks, is called the *Frobenius form* of A; two matrices are similar if and only if they have the same Frobenius form.

Two particularly useful properties of the Frobenius form are (1) the Frobenius form of a rational matrix is a rational matrix, and (2) a matrix is similar to its Frobenius form. You can obtain the Frobenius form with the `frobenius` command. (The Frobenius form is sometimes called the *rational canonical form,* though this term is also used by some authors for a possibly different element of the similarity class.)

Consider the matrix A defined here.

- `A:=matrix(4,4,1);`

A is a simple symmetric matrix.

Compute the Frobenius form of A.

- `F:=frobenius(A);`

Note that the result is assigned the name *F*. If *F* is similar to *A*, it is not at all obvious.

Compute the Smith forms of xI – A and xI – F.

- `smith(x-A,x);`
- `smith(x-F,x);`

Therefore, *A* and *F* are similar.

You can use a second parameter with `frobenius` *to obtain the transition matrix P satisfying P⁻¹AP = F.*

- `frobenius(A,'P');`
- `evalm(P);`
- `evalm(1/P &* A &* P);`

If *P* is an assigned variable, the single quotes may be necessary; otherwise not. (They do no harm in any case.)

Exercises on Smith Form and Frobenius Form

1. Let $p = 1 - x + x^2 - x^3 + x^4$ and $q = 1 - x + x^2$ have companion matrices A_{11} and A_{22}, respectively. Let *A* be the 6×6 matrix described in block form as $A = \begin{bmatrix} A_{11} & 0 \\ 0 & A_{22} \end{bmatrix}$. Let *C* be the companion matrix of *pq*. Use the Smith forms of $xI - A$ and $xI - C$ to show *A* and *C* are similar.

2. Use the Frobenius forms of the matrices *A* and *C* in Exercise 14 to show that they are similar.

3. Let $A = [a_{ij}]$ be the 6×6 matrix defined by $a_{ij} = \begin{cases} 1 \text{ if } i \geq j \\ j \text{ otherwise} \end{cases}$. Show that *A* is similar to its transpose.

4. It is a fact that every matrix is similar to its transpose. For a randomly generated 10×10 rational matrix *A*, show that *A* and its transpose have the same Frobenius form.

5. The `op` of a set is the sequence of elements in the set. The `op` of a nonnumerical sum is the sequence of summands. The `op` of a nonnumerical product is the sequence of factors. What is the `op` of an unindexed name of a matrix (that is, of the form *A*)? What is the `op` of an indexed name of a matrix (that is, of the form *A*[1])?

3.3 Applications

Systems of Linear Differential Equations

It is often necessary to solve systems of differential equations involving several functions. In matrix/vector form, a system of homogeneous first-order linear differential equations can be written $\mathbf{y}' = A\mathbf{y}$, where $\mathbf{y} = (y_1, y_2,$

..., y_n) is the vector of unknown functions, and the symbol $\mathbf{y}'$ is used for the vector of derivatives, $\mathbf{y}' = (y_1', y_2', ..., y_n')$.

For example, the system $\begin{cases} y_1' = 2y_1 + 3y_2 \\ y_2' = 3y_1 - 2y_2 \end{cases}$ can be written in matrix

form as $\mathbf{y}' = A\mathbf{y}$, where $A = \begin{bmatrix} 2 & 3 \\ 3 & -2 \end{bmatrix}$.

Define the matrix A.

• A:=matrix(2,2,[2,3,3,-2]);

Check the Jordan form of A.

• J:=jordan(A,Q);
• P:=inverse(Q);

The matrix A is diagonalizable, with transition matrix P satisfying $P^{-1}AP = J$.

The original system is equivalent to the "diagonal system" $\mathbf{z}' = \begin{bmatrix} -1 & 0 \\ 0 & 1 \end{bmatrix}\mathbf{z}$, with $\mathbf{y} = P\,\mathbf{z}$, $\mathbf{z} = (z_1, z_2)$. The matrix equation is equivalent to the

system $\begin{cases} z_1' = -z_1 \\ z_2' = z_2 \end{cases}$; hence the equations are said to be *unlinked*. They are

easily solved; the solutions are $z_1 = C_1 e^{-x}$ and $z_2 = C_2 e^x$. The solutions of the original system are given by $\mathbf{y} = P\,\mathbf{z}$.

Compute y.

• z:=vector([C1*exp(-x),C2*exp(x)]);
• y:=evalm(P &* z);

In some cases you may wish to use dsolve to solve the unlinked equations.

You could also use dsolve to solve systems of differential equations, but the technique just demonstrated is worth learning: It is useful in situations involving systems that *Maple* cannot handle automatically (recurrence relations, for example).

Consider next the example $\mathbf{y}' = A\mathbf{y}$, where $A = \begin{bmatrix} 2 & 2 & 1 \\ 1 & 3 & 4 \\ -1 & -2 & -2 \end{bmatrix}$.

Define the matrix A.

• A:=matrix(3,3,[2,2,1,1,3,4,-1,-2,-2]);

A is not diagonalizable, but it is triangularizable.

Find an upper-triangular matrix T similar to A and an associated transition matrix.

Use jordan *to find T and a transition matrix P.*

• T:=jordan(A,Q);
• P:=inverse(Q);

The system $\mathbf{z}' = T\mathbf{z}$ is now equivalent to the original system $\mathbf{y}' = A\mathbf{y}$.

This system can be solved using manual back-substitution. (You may want to ensure that t is not an alias before you use the following code.[8] The symbol t was used as an alias for several RootOfs earlier.)

Set up the required vectors.
- `z:=vector([z1,z2,z3]);`
- `Tz:=evalm(T &* z);`

If any of the entries z_1, z_2, or z_3 have been assigned, they will have to be unassigned before defining **z**.

Solve for z_3.
- `dsolve(D(z)(t)[3]=Tz(t)[3],z(t)[3]);`
- `assign(");`
- `_C1:=C1;`

The object of assigning $\_C1 = C1$ is to avoid having *Maple* use the same constant in the solution of z_2.

Solve for z_2.
- `dsolve(D(z)(t)[2]=Tz(t)[2],z(t)[2]);`
- `assign(");`
- `_C2:=C2;`

Note that *Maple* did not reuse $\_C1$; it will if $\_C1$ is not assigned, yielding a less general solution.

Solve for z_1.
- `dsolve(D(z)(t)[1]=Tz(t)[1],z(t)[1]);`
- `assign(");`
- `_C3:=C3;`

In this case, the introduction of $C3$ is for purely aesthetic reasons.

The solutions of the original system $\mathbf{y}' = A\mathbf{y}$ are now given by $\mathbf{y}(t)$, where $\mathbf{y} = P\mathbf{z}$.
- `y:=evalm(P &* z);`

It is generally a good idea to check the solutions. However, note that you will have to convert the entries of $y(t)$, which are expressions, to functions in order to use D for the check. You can do this with the command `y:=map(unapply,y(t),t)`.

It would be wise to unassign z_1, z_2, and z_3 at this point. If you do not, be sure to do so before you reuse the symbols with D. Or, if you are finished with your calculations, you may find it easier to quit the current session and begin a fresh one.

Exercises on Systems of Linear Differential Equations
In Exercises 1–4, solve the system of linear differential equations.

1. $\mathbf{y}' = A\mathbf{y}$, where $A = [a_{ij}]$ is given by $a_{ij} = i + j$

---

[8]The command `alias(t=t)` will ensure it.

2.
$$\begin{cases} y_1' = y_2 + y_4 \\ y_2' = y_1 + y_3 \\ y_3' = y_2 + y_4 \\ y_4' = y_1 + y_3 \end{cases}$$

3. $\mathbf{y}' = B\mathbf{y}$, where

$$B = \begin{bmatrix} 1 & -2 & -2 & -2 & -2 \\ 2 & 6 & 4 & 4 & 4 \\ -3 & -6 & -6 & -10 & -10 \\ 1 & 2 & 3 & 6 & 1 \\ 1 & 2 & 3 & 4 & 9 \end{bmatrix}$$

4. $\mathbf{y}' = C\mathbf{y}$, where

$$C = \begin{bmatrix} -205 & -409 & -613 & -817 & -1021 & -1225 \\ 494 & 986 & 1479 & 1972 & 2465 & 2958 \\ -662 & -1323 & -1986 & -2648 & -3310 & -3972 \\ 539 & 1078 & 1618 & 2156 & 2695 & 3234 \\ -272 & -544 & -816 & -1087 & -1360 & -1632 \\ 70 & 140 & 210 & 280 & 351 & 421 \end{bmatrix}$$

Problems on Systems of Linear Differential Equations

1. A linear differential equation can be solved by setting up an equivalent system of first-order differential equations. The process is simple yet effective and is important in the theory of differential equations.

   Consider the second-order differential equation

   $$y''(t) + y'(t) + 2y(t) = \mathbf{e}^t$$

   The solution process depends on the simple trick of introducing additional temporary variables $u_1 = y$ and $u_2 = y'$. With this substitution, the original equation is now equivalent to the system

   $$u_1' = u_2$$
   $$u_2' = -2\,u_1 - u_2 + \mathbf{e}^t$$

In matrix/vector form, this is simply $\mathbf{u}' = M\mathbf{u} + \mathbf{k}$, where

$$M = \begin{bmatrix} 0 & 1 \\ -2 & -1 \end{bmatrix}, \mathbf{u} = (u_1, u_2), \mathbf{u}' = (u_1', u_2'), \mathbf{k} = (0, \mathbf{e}^t)$$

The solution to this matrix/vector equation can be obtained by finding an upper-triangular matrix T similar to M that triangularizes M. If $T = P^{-1}MP$, then the original equation is equivalent to the upper-triangular system $\mathbf{y}' = T\mathbf{y} + P^{-1}\mathbf{k}$.

Solve the system $\mathbf{y}' = T\mathbf{y} + P^{-1}\mathbf{k}$ by back-substitution, using `dsolve` as required, and find $\mathbf{u} = P\mathbf{y}$.

The solution y_g can be written in the form $y_g = y_{Re} + y_{Im}\mathbf{i}$. Then

$$y'' + y' + 2y = \mathbf{e}^t$$

therefore

$$(y_{Re}'' + y_{Re}' + 2y_{Re}) + (y_{Im}'' + y_{Im}' + 2y_{Im})\mathbf{i} = \mathbf{e}^t$$

It follows that

$$y_{Re}'' + y_{Re}' + 2y_{Re} = \mathbf{e}^t$$

and

$$y_{Im}'' + y_{Im}' + 2y_{Im} = 0$$

The desired solution is most likely y_{Re}, which is obtained by applying `evalc(Re())` to y_g. Find y_{Re}.

2. Scientists in Elpmis have experimentally determined that the local populations $r(t)$ and $f(t)$ of rabbits and foxes, respectively, are related by the differential equations

$$\begin{cases} r'(t) = \dfrac{r(t)}{75} - \dfrac{f(t)}{150} \\[2mm] f'(t) = \dfrac{r(t)}{75} - \dfrac{f(t)}{300} \end{cases}$$

a. Find the (real) approximate populations $r(t)$ and $f(t)$ in floating-point form at time $t = 10$, 20, and 100, assuming that each is one thousand at time $t = 0$.

b. Repeat the problem assuming that there are 2000 rabbits and 1000 foxes at time $t = 0$.

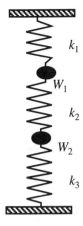

Figure 3-1

3. Engineers in Spring City are interested in the system pictured in Figure 3-1. Assume that the three springs are linear and massless, and that the weight W_2 is pulled down from its equilibrium position and released. The motion of the weights can be analyzed using Newton's second law of motion and Hooke's law. The equations governing the motion are

$$\frac{w_1 y_1''(t)}{g} = -k_1 y_1(t) + k_2 [y_2(t) - y_1(t)]$$

and

$$\frac{w_2 y_2''(t)}{g} = -k_2 [y_2(t) - y_1(t)] - k_3 y_2(t)$$

where

- w_1 is the weight of W_1 in pounds,
- w_2 is the weight of W_2 in pounds,
- k_1 is Hooke's constant for the upper spring, in pounds per foot,
- k_2 is Hooke's constant for the middle spring, in pounds per foot,
- k_3 is Hooke's constant for the lower spring, in pounds per foot,
- $g = 32$ ft/sec^2,
- $y_1(t)$ and $y_2(t)$ are the positions of W_1 and W_2 at time t relative to their equilibrium positions, and
- $y_1'(0) = y_2'(0) = 0$.

Convert the second-order system to an equivalent first-order system, and solve for $y_1(t)$ and $y_2(t)$, given the following information: $y_1(0) = 10$, $y_2(0) = 12$, $w_1 = 32$, $w_2 = 32$, $k_1 = 12$, $k_2 = 10$, $k_3 = 12$.

The Exponential Function
[exponential, JordanBlock, sort]

From the elementary theory of infinite series, you probably know that the exponential function $\exp(x) = e^x$ has the series expansion

$$e^x = \sum_{i=0}^{\infty} \frac{1}{i!} x^i$$

As you probably also know, the exponential function arises in solving the class of differential equations of the form $y' = ay$. The general solution is given by $y = Ce^{ax}$.

It is a most interesting idea (which, surprisingly, poses no problems) to extend the definition of the exponential function—and many other functions that can be defined by convergent power series—to matrices. For a matrix A, the function $\mathbf{e}^{At}$ is defined by the series

$$\mathbf{e}^{At} = \sum_{i=0}^{\infty} \frac{I}{i!}(At)^i = I + At + \frac{(At)^2}{2!} + \frac{(At)^3}{3!} + \cdots$$

If $Y(t)$ is a matrix of functions, $Y(t) = [y_{ij}(t)]$, the derivative $Y'(t)$ of $Y(t)$ is defined to be the matrix $[y_{ij}'(t)]$ of derivatives. The interest in the matrix exponential function is motivated by the fact that if $Y = Y(t)$ is a column of functions, and if A is a scalar matrix, then the matrix equation $Y' = AY$ has $Y = \mathbf{e}^{At}$ as a solution.

If A is the diagonal matrix $\text{diag}(\lambda_1, \ldots, \lambda_n)$, then it is easy to see that

$$\mathbf{e}^{At} = \begin{bmatrix} \mathbf{e}^{\lambda_1 t} & 0 & . & . & . & & 0 \\ 0 & \mathbf{e}^{\lambda_2 t} & . & . & & . & 0 \\ . & & . & & & & . \\ & & & . & & & 0 \\ 0 & 0 & . & . & . & & \mathbf{e}^{\lambda_n t} \end{bmatrix}$$

As it happens, if $P^{-1}AP = B = \text{diag}(\lambda_1, \ldots, \lambda_n)$, then $A = PBP^{-1}$, $A^2 = PB^2P^{-1}$, $\ldots$, and ultimately $\mathbf{e}^{At} = P\mathbf{e}^{Bt}P^{-1}$, that is,

$$\mathbf{e}^{At} = P \begin{bmatrix} \mathbf{e}^{\lambda_1 t} & 0 & . & . & . & & 0 \\ 0 & \mathbf{e}^{\lambda_2 t} & . & . & & . & 0 \\ . & & . & & & & . \\ & & & . & & & 0 \\ 0 & 0 & . & . & . & & \mathbf{e}^{\lambda_n t} \end{bmatrix} P^{-1}$$

Hence, if A is diagonalizable, the exponential function can be computed. A slightly more complicated analysis allows the calculation of $\mathbf{e}^{At}$ if its Jordan form can be computed.

Let S be a scalar matrix $S = \lambda I$, say, and let N be a matrix of the same size that has ones on the main superdiagonal and zeros elsewhere.

$$S = \begin{bmatrix} \lambda & . & . & . & 0 \\ 0 & \lambda & . & . & 0 \\ . & & . & & \\ . & & & . & \\ 0 & . & . & . & \lambda \end{bmatrix}, \quad N = \begin{bmatrix} 0 & 1 & . & . & 0 \\ 0 & 0 & 1 & . & . & 0 \\ . & & & & \\ & & & & 1 \\ 0 & . & . & . & 0 \end{bmatrix}$$

Then

$$J = S + N = \begin{bmatrix} \lambda & 1 & . & . & & 0 \\ 0 & \lambda & 1 & . & . & 0 \\ . & & & . & & \\ & & & & \lambda & 1 \\ 0 & . & . & . & & \lambda \end{bmatrix}$$

is a simple Jordan block, and every simple Jordan block is of this type.

You can generate simple Jordan blocks in *Maple* with the JordanBlock command.

This generates the simple 3 × 3 Jordan block with k on the diagonal. It is frequently denoted $J_3(k)$.

- J:=JordanBlock(k,3);

The first argument specifies the diagonal entry; the second specifies the size.

With S and N as defined, the exponential $\mathbf{e}^{Jt}$ is the sum of terms of the form

$\dfrac{1}{m!}(S + N)^m t^m$. The products $N^i S^{m-i}$ are then of interest because, by

the Binomial Theorem, $J^m = \displaystyle\sum_{i=0}^{m} \binom{m}{i} N^i S^{m-i}$. (Note that because S is a

scalar matrix, S commutes with all other matrices, and therefore the Binomial Theorem does apply.) Because S^{m-i} is the scalar matrix $\lambda^{m-i} I$, the product $N^i S^{m-i}$ is $\lambda^{m-i} N^i$.

Define N and S.

- N:=JordanBlock(0,3);
- S:=diag(k,k,k);

Calculate the first few powers of N.

- seq(evalm(N^i),i=0..3);

The superdiagonal of ones moves up one level each time the exponent increases, until it is gone. This behavior holds for all m.

The powers $(Jt)^m$ are now easily calculated using the Binomial Theorem.

This calculates the first few powers of Jt.

- `J:=S + N;`
- `Q:=seq(evalm((J*t)^i/``.i.`!`),i=0..5);`

Note that $(Jt)^0$ evaluates to 1 rather than I. *Maple* treats I and 1 in the same way in matrix sums.

Sum the powers.

- `i:='i';`
- `sum('Q[i]',i=1..6);`
- `evalm(");`

The output may be easier to grasp if it is sorted into standard form.

Sort the output, if necessary.

- `map(sort,");`

Can you make any sense of the output? All the terms seem to be related to truncated exponentials.

You can use *Maple*'s built-in `exponential` command to compute e^{Jt}.

Compute e^{Jt} *with* `exponential`.

- `exponential(J,t);`

Note that the first argument to the `exponential` command is the matrix; the second is the variable.

The output may vary from session to session; you may want to `sim-plify` it. If all is well, you will have $e^{kt}I + e^{kt}Nt + \frac{1}{2}e^{kt}N^2t^2$. Notice that this is a multiple, by a function, of a polynomial in t with matrix coefficients.

Maple's computation of the exponential e^{At} is not restricted to Jordan blocks. It can perform the computation for any matrix for which it can calculate the eigenvalues; that is the necessary prerequisite to finding the Jordan form, which is a block diagonal matrix with Jordan blocks on the diagonal. Notice that if J is the Jordan form of A, with $J = P^{-1}AP$, then $e^{At} = Pe^{Jt}P^{-1}$. It follows that the exponential of A is not likely to be as orderly as the exponential of J.

Exercises on the Exponential Function
1. Compute the exponential of the $n \times n$ analog of the Jordan block J that is treated in the above example, for each $n = 4\ldots6$.
2. Compute the exponential e^{Bt} of the 4×4 matrix $B = [b_{ij}]$, defined by $b_{ij} = 1$.
3. Compute the exponential e^{Ct} of the 4×4 matrix $C = [c_{ij}]$, where $c_{ij} = \begin{cases} i \text{ if } i > j \\ 0 \text{ if } i \le j \end{cases}$.

4. Compute the Jordan form J of the matrix C in Exercise 3, and a transition matrix P satisfying $P^{-1}CP = J$. Compare $P^{-1}e^{Ct}P$ and e^{Jt}.

Problems on the Exponential Function

1. It was noted in the discussion of the exponential that e^{At} is a solution of the matrix equation $Y' = AY$. Let $A = [a_{ij}]$ be the 4×4 matrix A defined by $a_{ij} = \begin{cases} i \text{ if } i < j \\ 0 \text{ if } i \geq j \end{cases}$. Use the matrix exponential to solve $Y' = AY$.

2. Find a system of first-order differential equations equivalent to the fourth-order equation $y^{(4)} - 6y^{(3)} + 13y'' + 4 = 0$. Use the exponential function to solve this system of first-order equations.

3. Use the matrix exponential to solve Problem 2 of the previous section, Systems of Linear Differential Equations (the rabbits and foxes problem).

4. Use the matrix exponential to solve Problem 3 of the previous section, Systems of Linear Differential Equations (the springs and weights problem).

Systems of Recurrence Relations
[rsolve]

A linear recurrence relation of length m is a fixed linear relation between the ith term of a sequence and the m terms immediately preceding it. Linear recurrence relations are also called *difference equations*.

A simple example of a recurrence relation is given by the equation $f(n + 1) = 2f(n)$. It is satisfied by the function $f(n) = 2^n$. The sequence $f(0)$, $f(1)$, ..., $f(n)$, is clearly determined by the value $f(0)$ and the relation $f(n + 1) = 2f(n)$. The general solution is $f(n) = C2^n$.

You can solve linear recurrence relations in *Maple* with the rsolve command. For example, to solve the recurrence relation $f(n + 1) = f(n)$ in *Maple*, you can proceed as follows:

You use rsolve *to solve a linear recurrence relation.*

• rsolve(f(n+1)=f(n),f);
The solution is determined by $f(0)$.

Often, it is necessary to solve systems of linear difference equations. The situation is analogous to that for differential equations.

Diagonalization and triangularization can also be used to solve some systems of linear recurrence relations. Consider the system

$$\begin{cases} f_1(n + 1) = f_1(n) - 2f_2(n) \\ f_2(n + 1) = f_1(n) + 4f_2(n) \end{cases}$$

In matrix/vector form, this is simply $\mathbf{f}(n + 1) = M\,\mathbf{f}(n)$, where $\mathbf{f} = (f_1, f_2)$ and $M = \begin{bmatrix} 1 & -2 \\ 1 & 4 \end{bmatrix}$. From this perspective, it is clear that if $\mathbf{f}(0)$ is known, then $\mathbf{f}(n) = M^n\,\mathbf{f}(0)$ for all $n \geq 0$; however, this does not give the most useful solution. The following gives the individual functions f_i in closed form.

Enter the matrix M.

- `M:=matrix(2,2,[1,-2,1,4]);`

Find the Jordan form J of M and an associated transition matrix.

- `J:=jordan(M,Q);`
- `P:=inverse(Q);`

The matrix P satisfies $P^{-1}MP = J$.

Solve the matrix system $\mathbf{g}(n + 1) = J\mathbf{g}(n)$.

- `g1:=n->C1*2^n;`
- `g2:=n->C2*3^n;`
- `g:=vector([g1,g2]);`

It is convenient to define g_1 and g_2 as functions. The vector $\mathbf{g}$ gives the general solution of the diagonal system; all particular solutions are obtained by varying the constants C_1 and C_2.

Find the solution of the original system.

- `f:=evalm(P &* g);`

Note that the components of $\mathbf{f}$ are functions.

Check the solution.

- `f[1](n+1)-f[1](n)+ 2*f[2](n);`
- `simplify(");`

The difference is 0; therefore, f_1 is a solution—you may wish to check f_2 as well.

    In some cases the expressions may be too complicated for *Maple* to simplify to 0; in that event, you can check the value of the difference for several values of n.

    If $\mathbf{f}$ contains complex entries, we let $\mathbf{f} = \mathbf{f}_{Re} + i\mathbf{f}_I$, where $\mathbf{f}_{Re}$ and $\mathbf{f}_{Im}$ are real vectors. Then $\mathbf{f}_{Re}$ and $\mathbf{f}_{Im}$ both satisfy the original equation $F(n + 1) = MF(n)$. For example, consider the system $\mathbf{f}(n + 1) = M\mathbf{f}(n)$, where $M = \begin{bmatrix} -7 & -13 \\ 3 & 5 \end{bmatrix}$.

Enter the matrix M.

- `M:=matrix(2,2,[-7,-13,3,5]);`

Compute the Jordan form of M and an associated transition matrix.

- `J:=jordan(M,Q);`
- `P:=inverse(Q);`

The matrix P satisfies $P^{-1}MP = J$.

Solve the matrix system $\mathbf{h}(n + 1) = J\mathbf{h}(n)$.

- `h1:=n->C1*J[1,1]^n;`
- `h2:=n->C2*J[2,2]^n;`
- `h:=vector([h1,h2]);`

The vector **h**(*n*) gives the general (complex) solution of the diagonal system. You should check the solution.

Solve for **f**$_g$.

- f[g]:=n->evalm(P&*h(n));

If you get an error message, unassign **f** and re-execute the command.

The vector **f**$_g$(*n*) is the general complex solution of the system **f**(*n* + 1) = *M***f**(*n*). However, in most cases, real solution vectors are desired and can be obtained.

Compute the real and imaginary components of **f**.

- f[Re]:=n->map(evalc@Re,f[g](n));
- f[Im]:=n->map(evalc@Im,f[g](n));

Sometimes the expressions in **f** may be too complicated for *Maple* to separate; the real or imaginary part may be returned incorrectly as the original complex number or as 0. (The @ symbol is used for function composition in *Maple*.)

You may wish to verify the solutions.

- evalm(f[Re](n+1)-M &* f[Re](n));
- map(simplify,");

The difference should be 0, but the result doesn't look much like it—it is too complicated for *Maple* to simplify. You can try using particular values for *n* and simplifying the result; of course, that gives only a probabilistic verification. Perhaps you can prove the validity of the approach in general.

It is not necessary that the coefficient matrix of a system **f**(*n* + 1) = *M***f**(*n*) of linear recurrence relations be diagonalizable in order to solve for f_1 and f_2 in closed form. This can be done from triangular form using back-substitution. For example, consider the system **f**(*n* + 1) = *M***f**(*n*), where **f** and *M* are defined by **f** = (f_1, f_2) and $M = \begin{bmatrix} 2 & 1 \\ -1 & 4 \end{bmatrix}$.

Enter the coefficient matrix M.

- M:=matrix(2,2,[2,1,-1,4]);

Use jordan *to find an upper triangular matrix J similar to M and a transition matrix P.*

- J:=jordan(M,Q);
- P:=inverse(Q);

The system **h**(*n* + 1) = *J***h**(*n*) is now equivalent to the original system, with the addendum that **f** = *P***h**.

Be sure **h**$_1$ *and* **h**$_2$ *are unassigned and then define* **h** *and J***h**.

- h1:='h1';h2:='h2';
- h:=vector([h1,h2]);
- Jh:=evalm(J &* h);

The system **h**(*n* + 1) = *J***h**(*n*) *is upper-triangular—solve for* **h**[2].

- rsolve(h[2](n+1)=Jh[2](n),h[2]);

Note that the solution is returned as an expression involving the undetermined constant $h_2(0)$. If the constant retains this name, the solution cannot be called h_2. If you get an error message here, unassign h_1 and h_2 and re-execute the command.

Use subs *to replace* $h_2(0)$
by C2. Convert the expres-
sion to a function and
assign it the name h_2.

- `h2:=unapply(subs(h2(0)=C2,"),n);`
The function h_2 is determined up to the arbitrary constant $C2 = h_2(0)$.

Because h_2 *is known, you*
can now determine h_1.

- `rsolve(h[1](n+1)=Jh[1](n),h[1]);`
The solution is returned as an expression involving $C2$ and the undetermined constant $h_1(0)$. Before you can use h_1 for the name of either the expression or the associated function, you must rename the constant.

Use subs *to replace* $h_1(0)$
by C1. Convert the expres-
sion to a function and
assign it the name h_1.

- `h1:=unapply(subs(h1(0)=C1,"),n);`
The function h_1 is now determined, up to the arbitrary constants $C1 = h_2(0)$ and $C2 = h_1(0)$.

Now compute $\mathbf{f} = P\mathbf{h}$.

- `f:=evalm(P &* h);`

You can now see $\mathbf{f}$(n) *by*
applying $\mathbf{f}$ *to n.*

- `f(n);`

Verify the solution.

- `evalm(f(n+1)- M &* f(n));`
The difference should be zero. Perhaps `simplify` will do the trick.

Apply `simplify`.

- `map(simplify,");`
If this does not return 0, you may want to perform a probabilistic check by simplifying $\mathbf{f}(n + 1) - M\mathbf{f}(n)$ for a few values of n.

Problems on Systems of Recurrence Relations

1. A group of environmentalists in Elpmis are concerned that two species may be endangered and are attempting to determine the stability of the species' populations. Their research shows that the populations interact and change from year to year according to the recurrence relations $\mathbf{p}(n + 1) = M\mathbf{p}(n)$, where

$$\mathbf{p} = (p_1, p_2) \, , M = \begin{bmatrix} 1/100 & -1/200 \\ 1/200 & -1/300 \end{bmatrix}$$

   a. If the current populations are given by $\mathbf{p}(0) = (1{,}000{,}000, 1{,}000{,}000)$, determine the approximate populations (in floating-point form) for each of the next ten years.

b. No reliable estimates of current populations are available. Find the general solution of the system $\mathbf{p}(n + 1) = M\mathbf{p}(n)$ and use it to investigate the possible future populations of the species depending on the current populations. What do you predict for the future?

2. The populations of three species in year n have been determined to be related by the recurrence relations $\mathbf{p}(n + 1) = M\mathbf{p}(n)$, where

$$\mathbf{p} = (p_1, p_2, p_3) \quad \text{and} \quad M = \begin{bmatrix} 1 & 1 & 0 \\ -1 & 2 & 1 \\ -1 & -1 & 4 \end{bmatrix}$$

Solve for $p_1(n)$, $p_2(n)$ and $p_3(n)$ in general. Based on your solution (and the assumption that none of the populations is currently negative), what is your projection for the futures of these species?

Quadratic Forms: The Principal Axis Theorem

For some geometric applications, it is highly desirable to work in orthogonal coordinate systems; when this is the case, orthogonal diagonalization is preferred. In this section, we consider one such application taken from analytic geometry: quadratic forms. In the eighteenth and nineteenth centuries, attempts to find a standardized form for quadratic forms in several variables provided impetus for the initial work with eigenvalues and eigenvectors.

Consider the expression $ax + 2bxy + cy^2$. It is called a *quadratic form* in x and y. This quadratic form can also be written as the matrix product XMX^T, where $M = \begin{bmatrix} a & b \\ b & c \end{bmatrix}$ and $X = [x,y]$.[9] In general, the expression

$$\sum_{i=1}^{n} a_{ij}x_i x_j \quad \text{(with } a_{ii} \neq 0, \, i = 1...n)$$ is a quadratic form in $x_1, x_2, ..., x_n$; it also

can be written in the form XMX^T, and the coefficients can be chosen so that the matrix M is symmetric. (You can easily verify this using *Maple* for, say, $n = 3$.)

An equation of the form $\sum_{i=1}^{n} a_{ij}x_i x_j = d$ is called a quadratic equation.

You have probably studied such equations—at least in the case $n = 2$, with $a_{ij} = 0$ if $i \neq j$. Familiar examples would probably include the ellipse $ax^2 + by^2 = 1$ and hyperbola $ax^2 - by^2 = 1$ (a, $b > 0$). You may or may not have studied

---

[9]In *Maple*, the product XMX^T is a 1×1 matrix, so some care will be required—the quadratic form would be XMX^T [1,1].

equations of the more general form $ax^2 + 2bxy + cy^2 = d$. However, this is easy to do in matrix form.

Consider the matrix equation $XMX^T = d$ (where we temporarily take the liberty of dropping the distinction between a 1×1 matrix and a scalar). If the coefficients are chosen so that the coefficient matrix M is symmetric—which is always possible by redefining the coefficients a_{ij} so that $a_{ij} = (a_{ij} + a_{ji})/2$—then M is orthogonally diagonalizable and there exists an orthogonal matrix P for which $P^{-1}MP$ is diagonal.

Because P is orthogonal, $P^{-1} = P^T$, and the equation $XMX^T = d$ can be rewritten as $(XP)(P^TMP)(P^TX^T) = d$. The substitution $Y = XP$ gives an orthogonal coordinate transformation; in the new coordinate system, the original equation becomes $YDgY^T = d$, where $Dg = \text{diag}(\lambda_1, \lambda_2, \ldots, \lambda_n)$ is a diagonal matrix with eigenvalues $\lambda_1, \lambda_2, \ldots, \lambda_n$. The associated quadratic equation is then $\displaystyle\sum_{i=1}^{n} \lambda_i y_i^2 = d$ (we will refer to this as the standard form of the quadratic).

The graphs of quadratic equations in standard form are well known in 2- and 3-space; the Principal Axis Theorem states that all quadratic equations in 2- and 3-space have graphs of these known types.

Exercises on Quadratic Forms

In Exercises 1–3, find the standard form of the quadratic equation in y_1-y_2 coordinates. Solve for y_2 and plot the graph in 2-space.

1. $3x_1^2 - 8x_1x_2 - 3x_2^2 = 1$
2. $x_1x_2 = 1$
3. $5x_1^2 + 6x_1x_2 + 3x_2^2 = 8$
4. Find the standard form of the quadratic equation
   $x_1^2 + x_2^2 + x_3^2 - 2x_1x_2 - 2x_1x_3 - 2x_2x_3 = 3$ in y_1-y_2-y_3 coordinates. Describe the graph.

Exercises 5–7 ask for 3-dimensional plots of quadratic equations. If J is the Jordan form of the matrix of the given quadratic, you can use

- `sum('J[i,i]*(y.i)^2',i=1..3)=d;`

to get the equation in standard form, where d is the constant on the right-hand side of the original equation. (Note the single quotes in the sum; also, recall that sum will not accept an assigned index variable.)

In each case, after finding the equivalent equation Eq in standard form, you can use

- `s:=solve(Eq,y3);`
- `r:= 5;`
- `plot3d({s},y1=-r..r,y2=-r..r);`

to get the plot. Some experimentation with the range (specified by r) may be required to get the desired result. In any case, the pieces of the plot may not fit together exactly—this depends on the values of y_1 and y_2 that *Maple* chooses to calculate the graph.

In Exercises 5–7, find the standard form of the quadratic equation in y_1-y_2-y_3 coordinates. Make a 3-dimensional plot of the graph.

5. $23x_1^2 + 50x_2^2 + 2x_3^2 - 72x_1x_3 = 50$

6. $68x_1^2 + 50x_2^2 + 82x_3^2 + 48x_1x_3 = 500$

7. $9x_1^2 + 6x_2^2 + 5x_3^2 - 4x_1x_2 = 500$

4 Linear Transformations

Many important functions between vector spaces are linear transformations. (A function T from a vector space U to a vector space V is a *linear transformation* if $T(\mathbf{u}_1 + \mathbf{u}_2) = T(\mathbf{u}_1) + T(\mathbf{u}_2)$ and $T(k\mathbf{u}) = kT(\mathbf{u})$, for all vectors $\mathbf{u}$, $\mathbf{u}_1$, and $\mathbf{u}_2$ in U, and all scalars k.) For example, if V is an n-dimensional vector space with basis $\mathbf{B}$, then the function $\mathbf{v} \rightarrow (\mathbf{v})_\mathbf{B}$ that takes every vector $\mathbf{v}$ to its coordinate vector $(\mathbf{v})_\mathbf{B}$ with respect to the basis $\mathbf{B}$ is a linear transformation from V to $\Re^n$. If V is an inner product space and U is a subspace, then the function $\mathbf{v} \rightarrow \text{proj}_U(\mathbf{v})$ is a linear transformation from V to U (or V to V). If A is an $m \times n$ matrix and U is a subspace of $\Re^n$, the function $\mathbf{v} \rightarrow A\mathbf{v}$ is a linear transformation from U to $\Re^m$.

4.1 Linear Transformations in *Maple*

You can define a linear transformation in Maple using either an arrow-style or `proc`-style definition.

This defines a linear transformation from $\Re^3$ to $\Re^4$ with an arrow-style definition.

- `L:=x->vector([3*x[1]-4*x[2],`
- `» x[2]+3*x[3],3*x[1]+1/2*x[3],x[3]]);`

Note that the *Maple* definition of L does not restrict its domain to $\Re^3$—or even to vectors.

As defined, L cannot successfully be applied to vector expressions.

- `u:=vector(3,i->i);`
- `v:=vector(4,i->i!);`
- `L(u+v);`

You could use `L(evalm(u+v))` here so that L is applied to a vector.

Using a `proc`-style definition, you can define linear transformations that will function properly with vector/matrix expressions.

This defines the same linear transformation L: $\Re^5 \rightarrow \Re^4$ in such a way that it can be applied to vector/matrix expressions.

- `T:=proc(x)`
» `local y;`
» `y:=evalm(x);`
» `vector([3*y[1]-4*y[2],`
» `y[2]+3*y[3],3*y[1]+1/2*y[3],y[3]])`
» `end;`

Notice that *T* applies `evalm` to its own argument.

T can be applied to expressions involving either numeric or symbolic vectors and matrices.

- `u:=vector([5,-7,9]);`
- `v:=vector(3,i->v.i);`
- `M:=matrix(3,3,max);`
- `T(M &* u + k*v);`

Note that `(i -> v.i)(j)` evaluates to `vj`.

*Notice that **y** still has the value it had before the application of T—even though it was assigned a value in the definition of T.*

- `y;`

The value of *y* is not changed outside of the procedure, because *y* was declared to be a *local* variable—one whose definition is maintained only within the procedure.

EXERCISES 4.1 _____

1. Let $T:\Re^5 \rightarrow \Re^4$ be the linear transformation $T(x_1,x_2,x_3,x_4,x_5) = (x_1 + x_2 + x_3 + x_4 + x_5, x_1 + x_2 + x_3 + x_4, x_1 + x_2 + x_3, x_1 + x_2)$.
    a. Define the linear transformation *T* in *Maple* and verify that it satisfies the properties $T(\mathbf{u}_1 + \mathbf{u}_2) = T(\mathbf{u}_1) + T(\mathbf{u}_2)$ and $T(k\mathbf{u}) = kT(\mathbf{u})$ for all 5-vectors $\mathbf{u}, \mathbf{u}_1$, and $\mathbf{u}_2$ and all scalars *k*.
    b. Let $\{\mathbf{e}_i\}_{i=1}^5$ be the standard basis for $\Re^5$. Calculate $T(\mathbf{e}_i)$, $i = 1...5$.
2. Let *U* be the subspace of $\Re^4$ spanned by the vectors $\mathbf{u}_1 = (1,1,1,0)$, $\mathbf{u}_2 = (1,1,0,0)$, and $\mathbf{u}_3 = (1,0,0,0)$. Let $T:\Re^4 \rightarrow \Re^4$ be the orthogonal projection $T(\mathbf{v}) = \text{proj}_U(\mathbf{v})$.
    a. Define the function *T* in *Maple*.
    b. Use vectors with unassigned entries and an unassigned symbolic scalar *k* to verify that *T* is a linear transformation.
    c. Verify that $T(T(\mathbf{v})) = T(\mathbf{v})$ for all **v**.
3. Find the orthogonal projection of the vector $\mathbf{v} = (1,2,3,4,5,6,7)$ onto the column space *U* of the 7×5 matrix $M = (m_{ij})$ defined by $m_{ij} = 1/(i + j)$. Verify that the orthogonal projection of $\Re^7$ onto *U* is a linear transformation. (See the previous exercise for a hint on how to do this with *Maple*.)
4. Let $\mathbf{B} = \{p_1, p_2, p_3, p_4, p_5, p_6\}$ be the basis of $\mathbf{P}_5$ defined by $p_i = (x - 2)^{i-1}$, $i = 1...6$. Let $T:\mathbf{P}_5 \rightarrow \Re^6$ be the function defined by $T(p) = (p)_{\mathbf{B}}$.
    a. Verify that **B** is a basis of $\mathbf{P}_5$.
    b. Verify that *T* is a linear transformation.
    c. Find $T(x^i)$ for $i = 0...5$.
    d. Find $T(a_0 + a_1x + \cdots + a_5x^5)$ in general.

5. Let $\mathbf{u}_1$, $\mathbf{u}_2$, ..., $\mathbf{u}_{i-1}$, $\mathbf{u}_{i+1}$, ..., $\mathbf{u}_n$ be fixed n-vectors. Let $L(\mathbf{u})$ be the determinant of the $n \times n$ matrix $[\mathbf{u}_1, \mathbf{u}_2, ..., \mathbf{u}_{i-1}, \mathbf{u}, \mathbf{u}_{i+1}, ..., \mathbf{u}_n]$. Then L is a linear transformation. Verify this for $n = 5$ and $i = 5$ by using vectors with undefined symbols as entries.

4.2 Matrices and Linear Transformations
[genmatrix]

Because any n-dimensional real vector space can be identified with $\mathfrak{R}^n$ (via the coordinates associated with a basis), linear transformations from $\mathfrak{R}^n$ to $\mathfrak{R}^m$ assume a special importance.

If A is an $m \times n$ matrix, then the function $T(\mathbf{v}) = A\mathbf{v}$ from $\mathfrak{R}^n$ to $\mathfrak{R}^m$ is clearly a linear transformation; such a linear transformation is called a *matrix transformation*. A fact crucial to understanding the theory of linear algebra is that *every* linear transformation $T{:}\mathfrak{R}^n{\to}\mathfrak{R}^m$ is a matrix transformation. The matrix A such that $A\mathbf{v} = T(\mathbf{v})$ is called the *standard matrix* of T.

This defines a particular linear transformation $T{:}\mathfrak{R}^6{\to}\mathfrak{R}^3$.

```
•  T:=
»  proc(x)
»  local y;
»  y:=evalm(x);
»  vector([y[1],y[2]+y[3],y[4]+y[5]+y[6]])
»  end;
```

You can determine the standard matrix of T by applying it to a vector with undefined entries.

```
•  v:=vector(6);
•  Tv:=T(v);
```
The result of applying T to $\mathbf{v}$ is assigned the name Tv, for future reference.

The matrix of T is easily determined from the expression Tv.

```
•  A:=matrix(3,6,
»  [1,0,0,0,0,0,
»  0,1,1,0,0,0,
»  0,0,0,1,1,1]);
```
The (i,j)-entry of A is the coefficient of $v[j]$ in the ith component of $T(\mathbf{v})$.

Alternatively, you might use the genmatrix command to have Maple compute the matrix A for you—especially if A is large.

```
•  genmatrix(
»  [Tv[1],Tv[2],Tv[3]],
»  [v[1],v[2],v[3],v[4],v[5],v[6]]);
```
Note that the first argument is the list of components of $T(\mathbf{v})$, and the second argument is the list of components of $\mathbf{v}$.

You may want to use the seq command with genmatrix.

```
•  genmatrix([seq(Tv[i],i=1..3)],
»  [seq(v[i],i=1..6)]);
```
This gives a compact form of the command.

*You can easily verify the equation T(**v**) = A**v** by evaluating T(**v**) – A**v**.*

- ```
evalm(T(v)-A &* v);
```
The zero difference verifies the identity.

*In general, the ith column vector of the standard matrix is T(**e**$_i$), where **e**$_i$ is the ith standard basis vector for $\Re^n$.*

- ```
for i to 6
```
» ```
do
```
» ```
  e[i]:=vector(6,proc(j)
```
» ```
  if i=j then 1 else 0 fi end);
```
» ```
od;
```

- ```
A:=augment(seq(T(e[i]),i=1..6));
```

*You can derive bases for the kernel and range of T from A.*

- ```
nullspace(A);
```
- ```
rref(transpose(A));
```
In the second calculation, the nonzero rows of the result are a basis for the range.[1]

   If a linear transformation $L$ is specified by a collection of equations $L(\mathbf{b}_i) = \mathbf{m}_i$, $i = 1...k$, where $\{\mathbf{b}_1,\mathbf{b}_2, ..., \mathbf{b}_k\}$ is a basis for $V$, you can easily create a *Maple* procedure that returns $L(\mathbf{v})$ for any vector **v** in $V$. Note that if $\mathbf{v} = a_1\mathbf{b}_1 + \cdots + a_k\mathbf{b}_k$, then $L(\mathbf{v}) = a_1\mathbf{m}_1 + \cdots + a_k\mathbf{m}_k$.

*Here are two collections $\mathbf{b}_1, ..., \mathbf{b}_5$ and $\mathbf{m}_1, ..., \mathbf{m}_5$ of vectors in $\Re^7$. The vectors $\mathbf{b}_1, ..., \mathbf{b}_5$ are a basis for the subspace V that they span.*

- ```
for j to 5
```
» ```
do
```
» ```
  b[j]:=vector(7,i->min(i,j))
```
» ```
od;
```
- ```
for j to 5
```
» ```
do
```
» ```
  m[j]:=vector(7,i->min(i+1,j+1))
```
» ```
od;
```

*If $\mathbf{v} = a_1\mathbf{b}_1 + \cdots + a_5\mathbf{b}_5$ is any vector in V, then $a_1, a_2, ..., a_5$ can be obtained by using row-reduction and back-substitution on the matrix $B = [\mathbf{b}_1, ..., \mathbf{b}_5, \mathbf{v}]$.*

- ```
B:=augment(seq(b[i],i=1..5));
```
- ```
v:=vector([1,7,9,4,2,2,2]);
```
- ```
rref(augment(B,v));
```
- ```
a:=backsub(");
```
The vector $\mathbf{a} = (a_1,a_2, ..., a_5)$ is the coordinate vector of **v** with respect to the basis **B**= $\{\mathbf{b}_1, ..., \mathbf{b}_5\}$. Recall that if a vector **v** lies outside of the span of $\mathbf{b}_1, ..., \mathbf{b}_5$, then this procedure will return an error message.

*L(**v**) is now given by $a_1\mathbf{v}_1 + \cdots + a_5\mathbf{v}_5 = M\mathbf{a}$, with $M = [\mathbf{m}_1, ..., \mathbf{m}_5]$.*

- ```
M:=augment(seq(m[i],i=1..5));
```
- ```
w:=evalm(M &* a);
```
Notice that the result is assigned the name **w**.

---

[1]*Maple* has a built-in `range` command that you can conveniently use here.
```

These steps can easily be combined into a procedure.

- `L:= x->`
  » `evalm(M &* backsub(rref(augment(B,x))));`

Note that L will apply the same steps that were applied to $\mathbf{v}$ to any vector $\mathbf{x}$. You may wish to verify this by comparing $L(\mathbf{v})$ with the vector $\mathbf{w}$.

Here is a basis for a subspace W of $\Re^7$ containing $\mathbf{m}_1, ..., \mathbf{m}_5$.

- `r:='r';`
- `for j to 5`
  » `do`
  » `c[j]:=vector(7,`
  » `  i->sum(r,r=max(j-i+1,0)..j))`
  » `od;`

- `C:=augment(seq(c[j],j=1..5));`

*If you desire the matrix of L with respect to **B** and **C**, you can compute it by row-reduction and back-substitution.*

- `rref(augment((C,M)));`
- `backsub(");`

Note that $M = [L(\mathbf{b}_1), ..., L(\mathbf{b}_5)]$, so the result is $[(L(\mathbf{b}_1))_{\mathbf{C}}, ..., (L(\mathbf{b}_5))_{\mathbf{C}}]$, the matrix of L with respect to **B** and **C**.

EXERCISES 4.2

1. For $i = 1...7$, let $\mathbf{b}_i = (b_{ij})$ and $\mathbf{c}_i = (c_{ij})$ be the 7-vectors defined by
   $$b_{ij} = \begin{cases} 0 \text{ if } i = j \\ 1 \text{ otherwise} \end{cases} \text{ and } c_{ij} = i + j - 1. \text{ Assume that } T \text{ is a linear transfor-}$$
   mation from $\Re^7$ to $\Re^7$ satisfying $T(\mathbf{b}_i) = \mathbf{c}_i$, $i = 1...7$. Define T in *Maple* and find its standard matrix.

2. Find the kernel and range of T (see Exercise 1).

3. Let $B = \{\mathbf{b}_1, ..., \mathbf{b}_6\}$ be the basis for $\Re^6$ defined by $\mathbf{b}_i = (b_{ij})$, $b_{ij} = \min(i,j)$. Define a procedure Crd that takes every vector $\mathbf{v}$ in $\Re^6$ to its **B**-coordinate vector. Verify that Crd is a linear transformation. You can do this with "symbolic vectors" **u** and **v**: show that both `Crd(u+v)-Crd(u)-Crd(v)` and `Crd(k*u)-k*Crd(u)` evaluate to zero. You may have to map `simplify` onto the result in the latter case.

4. Find the standard matrix of the linear transformation Crd (see Exercise 3).

5. Let $\mathbf{B} = \{\mathbf{b}_i\}_{i=1}^{6}$ be the basis of $\Re^6$, as in Exercise 3. Let W be the subspace of $\Re^9$ with basis $\mathbf{C} = \{\mathbf{c}_i\}_{i=1}^{6}$, where $\mathbf{c}_i = (c_{ij})$ is the 9-vector defined by $c_{ij} = \max(j - i + 1,1)$. Let $\mathbf{d}_i = (d_{ij})$ be the vectors of W defined by $d_{ij} = \min(i + 1, j + 1)$, $i = 1...6$. Let $L:\Re^6 \to \Re^9$ be the linear transformation determined by the equations $L(\mathbf{b}_i) = \mathbf{d}_i$, $i = 1...6$. Define a function T that takes the **B**-coordinate vector of any $\mathbf{v}$ in $\Re^6$ to the **C**-coordinate vector of $L(\mathbf{v})$. Verify that T is a linear transformation from $\Re^6$ to $\Re^6$.

6. Find the standard matrix of the linear transformation T (see Exercise 5).

7. Let $L:\Re^7 \to \Re^5$ be the linear transformation $L(\mathbf{x}) = A\mathbf{x}$, where $A = [a_{ij}]$ is the 5×7 matrix defined by $a_{ij} = i + j$. Find the general solution s[g] of the equation $L(\mathbf{x}) = (35,42,49,56,63)$ and use subs to obtain a particular solution s[p]. Find the general solution s[h] of the homogeneous equation $L(\mathbf{x}) = \mathbf{0}$. Verify that s[g] = s[p] + s[h].

4.3 Applications

Differential Equations
[dsolve, diff, D]

A linear transformation of particular importance is the differential operator $\mathbf{D}(\mathbf{f}) = \mathbf{f}'$. From elementary calculus we know that the differential operator $\mathbf{D}$ satisfies the properties

a. $\mathbf{D}(\mathbf{f} + \mathbf{g}) = \mathbf{D}(\mathbf{f}) + \mathbf{D}(\mathbf{g})$, and
b. $\mathbf{D}(k\mathbf{f}) = k\,\mathbf{D}(\mathbf{f})$

This is also true of the identity operator $\mathbf{D}^0 = \mathbf{I}$, the higher-order differential operators $\mathbf{D}^2 = \mathbf{D} \circ \mathbf{D}$, $\mathbf{D}^3 = \mathbf{D} \circ \mathbf{D} \circ \mathbf{D}$, ..., and all their linear combinations $\mathbf{L} = a_0\mathbf{I} + a_1\mathbf{D} + \cdots + a_m\mathbf{D}^m$ (it is common to write a_0 in place of $a_0\mathbf{I}$ in this notation, but this does not work well in *Maple*).

In this section we consider differential equations of the form

$$\mathbf{L}(y)(x) = \mathbf{f}(x) \tag{4.3.1}$$

where $\mathbf{L}$ is of the form

$$\mathbf{L} = a_0\mathbf{I} + a_1\,\mathbf{D} + \cdots + a_m\,\mathbf{D}^m \tag{4.3.2}$$

We assume that the function $\mathbf{f}(x)$ is continuous on some interval $[a,b]$ and that all the coefficients a_i are real. Note that (as for all linear transformations) the general solution $\mathbf{s}_g$ of the equation $\mathbf{L}(y)(x) = \mathbf{f}(x)$ has the form $\mathbf{s}_g = \mathbf{s}_p + \mathbf{s}_h$, where $\mathbf{s}_h$ is the general solution of the associated homogeneous equation $\mathbf{L}(y)(x) = 0$, and $\mathbf{s}_p$ is any particular solution of the equation $\mathbf{L}(y) = \mathbf{f}(x)$. This makes it particularly desirable to find a basis for the solution space of the associated homogeneous equation (in other words, the kernel of $\mathbf{L}$).

For example, consider the operator $\mathbf{L}$ defined by $\mathbf{L}(y) = \mathbf{D}(y) - y = y' - y$ and the equation $\mathbf{L}(y)(x) = x$. One particular solution of this equation is given by $\mathbf{s}_p(x) = -x - 1$, as you can easily verify by direct calculation. You may recall from calculus that the general solution of the equation $\mathbf{L}(y) = 0$ is given by $y(x) = Ce^x$. Hence, the general solution of the equation $\mathbf{D}(y) - y = x$ is given by $\mathbf{s}_g(x) = \mathbf{s}_p(x) + \mathbf{s}_h(x) = -x - 1 + Ce^x$.

The differential operator in Equation (4.3.2) is naturally associated with the polynomial $C(x) = a_0 + a_1x + \cdots + a_mx^m$. This polynomial—called the characteristic polynomial of **L**—is of particular importance in solving the homogeneous differential equation **L**$(y) = 0$. The operator **L** is frequently written as $C(\mathbf{D})$; if $C(x)$ has the factorization $C(x) = p_1(x)p_2(x)$ then $\mathbf{L} = C(\mathbf{D})$ has the factorization $\mathbf{L} = p_1(\mathbf{D})p_2(\mathbf{D})$. In particular, if

$$C(x) = \prod_{i=1}^{r} (x - r_i)^{e_i} \tag{4.3.3}$$

where $r_i \neq r_j$ if $i \neq j$, then $\mathbf{L} = a_0\mathbf{I} + a_1\mathbf{D} + \cdots + a_n\mathbf{D}^m$ has the factorization $\mathbf{L} =$

$$\prod_{i=1}^{r} (\mathbf{D} - r_i\mathbf{I})^{e_i} \,.$$

The solutions of the homogeneous equation **L**$(y) = 0$ are the linear combinations of the solutions of the r homogeneous equations $(\mathbf{D} - r_i\mathbf{I})^{e_i}(y) = 0$. From calculus, we know that Ce^{kx} is the general solution of the differential equation $(\mathbf{D} - k\mathbf{I})(y) = 0$. Hence, if the exponents $e_i = 1$ for all $i = 1\ldots r$ in Equation (4.3.3), then the solutions of the differential equation **L**$(y) = 0$ are the linear combinations $C_1e^{r_1x} + C_2e^{r_2x} + \cdots + C_me^{r_mx}$.

You can solve many differential equations in *Maple* with the `dsolve` command. *Maple* uses `D@@n` for $\mathbf{D}^n$, including `D@@0` for **I**. (You can use `D` in place of `D@@1` or `x->x` in place of `D@@0`. This notation works for functions; for other expressions, you can use the notation `diff(y(x),x$i)` for d^iy/dx^i ($i \geq 1$). You can also use `diff(y(x),x)` in place of `diff(y(x),x$1)`, but you cannot use `diff(y(x),x$0)` in place of `y(x)`.) The `D` notation is generally easier to use when it is applicable, but sometimes the `diff` notation is appropriate.

Consider the example $\mathbf{L} = \mathbf{D}^2 - 4\mathbf{D} + 3\mathbf{I} = (\mathbf{D} - \mathbf{I})(\mathbf{D} - 3\mathbf{I})$.

Because I is used for $\sqrt{-1}$, you may wish to alias `ID` *to* `D@@0`.

- `alias(ID=D@@0);`

If you choose not to do this, then use `D@@0` in place of `ID` in the following.

This defines $\mathbf{L} = \mathbf{D}^2 - 4\mathbf{D} + 3\mathbf{I}$.

- `L:=D@@2-4*D+3*ID;`

Note that *Maple* formats the output using $D^{(2)}$ and `ID`.

This defines the "factors" $\mathbf{L}_1 = (\mathbf{D} - \mathbf{I})$ *and* $\mathbf{L}_2 = (\mathbf{D} - 3\mathbf{I})$.

- `L1:=D-3*ID;`
- `L2:=D-ID;`

Note that you cannot use the notation `L[1]` for $\mathbf{L}_1$ here without destroying the definition of **L**.

This solves the homogeneous differential equation $\mathbf{L}(y) = 0$.

- `s[h]:=dsolve(L(y)(x)=0,y(x));`

Note that **L** is applied to y only—not to $y(x)$.

Compare this with the solutions of $\mathbf{L}_1(y) = 0$ *and* $\mathbf{L}_2(y) = 0$.

- `dsolve(L1(y)(x)=0,y(x));`
- `dsolve(L2(y)(x)=0,y(x));`

Note that the solutions of $\mathbf{L}(y) = 0$ are linear combinations of the solutions of $\mathbf{L}_1(y) = 0$ and $\mathbf{L}_2(y) = 0$. Also note that both solutions use the same symbol for an arbitrary constant, though the constants are not tied to each other.

Now consider the differential equation $\mathbf{L}(y) = x^2$, where $\mathbf{L}(y) = \mathbf{D}^2 - 4\mathbf{D} + 3\mathbf{I}$.

Use dsolve *to obtain the general solution.*

- `s[g]:=dsolve(L(y)(x)=x^2,y(x));`

The solution is completely general: all particular solutions are obtained by varying the parameters in the general solution s_g.

You can obtain particular solutions using subs.

- `s[p]:=subs(_C1=0,_C2=0,s[g]);`

All solutions are obtained by varying the parameters _C1 and _C2. Note that the two solutions obtained by substituting _C1 = 0, _C2 = 1 and _C1 = 1, _C2 = 0 are the solutions of the equations $y' - 3y = 0$ and $y' - y = 0$.

You can verify the relation $s_g = s_p + s_h$.

- `s[p]+s[h];`
- `s[g];`

The right-hand sides of the two equations are the same (except, perhaps, for their form).

The Wronskian
[unapply, rhs]
It is a theorem that the kernel of a differential operator of the form

$$\mathbf{L} = a_0\mathbf{I} + a_1\mathbf{D} + \cdots + a_m\mathbf{D}^m \quad (a_m \neq 0)$$

is an m-dimensional vector space. The Wronskian function (defined later) gives you a means of verifying that you have all the solutions.

Let $\mathbf{L} = \displaystyle\prod_{j=1}^{5}(\mathbf{D} - j\mathbf{I})$, so that the solution space of $\mathbf{L}(y) = 0$ has

dimension five.

This defines $\mathbf{L}$.

- `L:=`
» `(D-ID)@(D-2*ID)@(D-3*ID)@`
» `(D-4*ID)@(D-5*ID);`

This solves the differential equation $\mathbf{L}(y) = 0$.

- `s[h]:=dsolve(L(y)(x)=0,y(x));`

The solutions are the linear combinations of the basic solutions e^x, e^{2x}, e^{3x}, e^{4x}, and e^{5x}.

This puts the basic solutions into a list **LL**, *as expressions.*

- `subs(seq(_C.i=1,i=1..6),");`
- `LL:=[op(rhs("))];`

The `rhs` command gives the right-hand side of the equations; the `op` function returns the operands of the right-hand side—in this case the summands.

This uses unapply *to change the expressions in* **LL** *to functions, so that the* **D** *operator can be used.*

- `b:=map(unapply,LL,x);`

The `unapply` command converts an expression to a function. Here, `map` is used to convert all the entries of the list **LL**. You might wish to investigate these commands further in *Maple*'s help system.

The Wronskian function is the function $W(x)$ defined by

$$W(x) = \det(M)$$

where the matrix $M = [m_{ij}]$ is given by $m_{ij} = \mathbf{D}^{i-1}(\mathbf{b}[j])$. The matrix $M = M(x)$ is called the Wronskian matrix. If the components of **b** are linearly dependent, then the columns of the matrix M are linearly dependent and hence $W(x) = \det(M) = 0$ for every real x. It follows that $W(x) = 0$ as a function. In this case, the converse is true as well.[2] Hence, $W(x) = 0$ if and only if the entries of **b** are linearly dependent. The following procedure tests whether $W(0) = 0$.

Generate the Wronskian matrix.

- `M:=matrix(5,5,(i,j)->(D@@(i-1))(b[j]));`

It may seem that the definition has not been successful, but it will pay to test it.

Test the definition.

- `M(x);`

When a list, vector, or matrix of functions is applied to a number or symbol, the result is the list or array of values. This shows that all entries are properly defined, though this was perhaps not clear from the way *Maple* printed M.

Define the Wronskian function.

- `W:=x->det(M(x));`

Check $W(0)$.

- `W(0);`

Because $W(0) \neq 0$, the solutions $\mathbf{e}^x$, $\mathbf{e}^{2x}$, $\mathbf{e}^{3x}$, $\mathbf{e}^{4x}$, and $\mathbf{e}^{5x}$ are linearly independent. Because $\mathbf{s}_h$ has dimension five, it follows that every element of $\mathbf{s}_h$ is a linear combination of $\mathbf{e}^x$, $\mathbf{e}^{2x}$, $\mathbf{e}^{3x}$, $\mathbf{e}^{4x}$, and $\mathbf{e}^{5x}$.

[2] For more information, see, for example, Charles G. Cullen, *Linear Algebra and Differential Equations* (Boston: Prindle, Weber & Schmidt, 1979).

Initial Conditions

It is a theorem that, for any differential operator

$$L = a_0 I + a_1 D + \cdots + a_m D^m \quad (a_m \neq 0)$$

each vector $\mathbf{v} = (v_1, v_2, \ldots, v_m)$ in $\mathfrak{R}^m$ corresponds to a unique solution $\mathbf{s}$ satisfying $\mathbf{s}^{(i)}(0) = v_{i+1}$, $i = 0 \ldots m - 1$ (where $\mathbf{s}^{(0)} = \mathbf{s}$). This correspondence is also linear, so all solutions of the homogeneous equation $L(y) = 0$ can be found from any m solutions $\mathbf{s}_i$ that correspond to a basis for $\mathfrak{R}^m$. Earlier you found the basic solutions $\mathbf{e}^x$, $\mathbf{e}^{2x}$, $\mathbf{e}^{3x}$, $\mathbf{e}^{4x}$, and $\mathbf{e}^{5x}$ of the differential equation

$$L(y) = 0, \text{ for } L = \prod_{i=1}^{5} (D - i\mathbf{I}). \text{ Because } D^i(e^{jx}) = j^i e^{jx}, \text{ so that } D^i(e^{jx})(0) = j^i,$$

these solutions correspond (at $x = 0$) to the transpose of the Vandermonde matrix on 1,2,3,4,5. This matrix $V = M(0)$ is invertible, hence solutions corresponding to any vectors in $\mathfrak{R}^m$ are easily found from it. As an illustration, the solution $\mathbf{s}_1$ of $L(y) = 0$ corresponding to the vector $\mathbf{e}_1 = (1,0,0,0,0)$ is found in the following example. If the definitions of L, LL, and M are no longer active from the calculation of W in the previous section, you will have to reactivate them.

Define the matrix V.

- `V:=M(0);`

V^T is a Vandermonde matrix (enter `?vandermonde` if you want to review this topic).

You can review the definition of L with the `print` *command.*

- `print(L);`

You should get $L = \prod_{i=1}^{5} (D - i\mathbf{I})$; if not, redefine L.

Define the vector $\mathbf{e}_1 =$ *(1,0,0,0,0).*

- `e[1]:=vector([1,0,0,0,0]);`

If you find the solutions g_i corresponding to all the row vectors e_i of the identity matrix $\mathbf{I}_5$, then the solution corresponding to any vector $\mathbf{c} =$

$$(c_1, c_2, c_3, c_4, c_5) \text{ is simply } \sum_{i=1}^{5} c_i g_i.$$

Solve the equation $V\mathbf{x} = \mathbf{e}_1$.

- `rref(augment(V,e[1]));`
- `a:=backsub(");`

Note that $\mathbf{a}$ is the coefficient vector of $\mathbf{e}_1$ with respect to the column vectors of V.

Compute the solution (as an expression) corresponding to the vector $\mathbf{e}_1$.

- `s[expr]:=innerprod(vector(LL),a);`

Recall that $LL = [\ e^x, e^{2x}, e^{3x}, e^{4x}, e^{5x}\ ]$ is the list of basic solutions of $L(y)$ $= 0$.

Convert the expression to a function.

- `s[1]:=unapply(s[expr],x);`

The `unapply` command is used to convert an expression to the associated function; it was used earlier to create the list **b** that was then used to define the matrix *M*.

The solution $s_1(x)$ should now satisfy $D^i(s_1)(0) = \delta_{i0}$, $i = 0...4$.

- `[seq((D@@i)(s[1]),i=0..4)];`
- `"(0);`

The result should be [1,0,0,0,0].

You can solve differential equations with initial conditions directly as well, using `dsolve`. For example, if the initial conditions were $y^{(i)}(0) = C_i$, $i = 0...m - 1$, the syntax would be

- `dsolve({L(y)(x)=f(x),y(0)=C0,D(y)(0)=C1,...,`
- `» (D@@(m-1))(y)(0)= Cm},y(x));`

This also obtains the solution s_1 corresponding to $e_1 = (1,0,0,0,0)$.

- `dsolve({L(y)(x)=0,y(0)=1,D(y)(0)=0,`
- `» (D@@2)(y)(0)=0, (D@@3)(y)(0)=0,`
- `» (D@@4)(y)(0)=0},y(x));`

Compare the result with the value of **s** already obtained.

Exercises on Differential Equations

1. a. Solve the differential equations $(\mathbf{D}^2 - 3\mathbf{D} - 4\mathbf{I})(y) = e^x$ and $(\mathbf{D}^2 - 3\mathbf{D} - 4\mathbf{I})(y) = 0$.
    b. Compare the solutions of $(\mathbf{D}^2 - 3\mathbf{D} - 4\mathbf{I})(y) = 0$ with those of $(\mathbf{D} - 4\mathbf{I})(y) = 0$ and $(\mathbf{D} + \mathbf{I})(y) = 0$.

2. Assume $\mathbf{F} = \mathbf{D} - 2\mathbf{I}$ and $\mathbf{L} = \mathbf{F} \circ \mathbf{F} \circ \mathbf{F}$.
    a. Show that e^{2x}, xe^{2x}, and x^2e^{2x} are solutions of **L**.
    b. Use the Wronskian function to show that the solutions in part a are linearly independent. Can you conclude that they are a basis for the kernel of **L**?
    c. What do you conjecture about the solutions of $(\mathbf{D} - r)^f$ in general? Verify your conjecture for $\mathbf{F} \circ \mathbf{F} \circ \mathbf{F} \circ \mathbf{F} \circ \mathbf{F}$.

3. If the characteristic polynomial $\mathbf{C}(x)$ of a differential operator **L** has a complex root, then the factorization of $\mathbf{C}(x)$ over the reals has an irreducible real quadratic factor $(x + a)^2 + b^2$. If the factor $(x + a)^2 + b^2$ appears to a power $f \geq 1$ in the factorization over the reals of $\mathbf{C}(x)$, then the solutions of the equation $\mathbf{L}(y) = 0$ that are contributed by the factor $(\mathbf{D} + a\mathbf{I})^2 + b^2\mathbf{I})^f = (\mathbf{D}^2 + 2a\mathbf{D} + (a^2 + b^2)\mathbf{I})^f$ can be expressed as linear combinations of the solutions $e^{-ax}\sin(bx)$, $e^{-ax}\cos(bx)$, $xe^{-ax}\sin(bx)$, $xe^{-ax}\cos(bx)$, ..., $x^{f-1}e^{-ax}\sin(bx)$, and $x^{f-1}e^{-ax}\sin(bx)$.
    a. Define the linear operator $\mathbf{L} = ((\mathbf{D} + 2\mathbf{I})^2 + (3^2 + 2^2)\mathbf{I})^3$.
    b. Verify that $x^ie^{-2x}\sin(3x)$ and $x^ie^{-2x}\cos(3x)$ are solutions for $i = 0...2$.
    c. Use the Wronskian to verify that the six solutions are linearly independent (use `exp(-ax)` for e^{-ax}).
    d. Compare your solutions with the solutions returned by `dsolve`.

4. Let $\mathbf{L} = \mathbf{D}^3 - 6\mathbf{D}^2 + 11\mathbf{D} - 6\mathbf{I} = (\mathbf{D} - \mathbf{I})(\mathbf{D} - 2\mathbf{I})(\mathbf{D} - 3\mathbf{I})$.
    a. Find the solution space of the homogeneous differential equation $\mathbf{L}(y) = 0$.
    b. Find a basis for the vector space of part a.
    c. Find all solutions of the differential equation $\mathbf{L}(y) = e^{3x}$.
5. Let $p = x^5 + x^4 + x^3 + x^2 + x + 1$, and let $\mathbf{L}$ be the differential operator with characteristic polynomial p.
    a. Use the `factor` command to verify that p has an irreducible quadratic factor over the reals.
    b. Find all solutions of the differential equation $\mathbf{L}(y) = 0$.
    c. Find the solution z of $\mathbf{L}(y) = 0$ satisfying the initial conditions $z(0) = 1$ and $z^{(i)}(0) = 0$, $i = 1\ldots4$.
    d. Find the solution z of $\mathbf{L}(y) = 0$ satisfying the initial conditions $z^{(i)}(0) = 0$, $i = 0\ldots4$, where $z^{(0)} = z$.
6. Let $\mathbf{L}$ be the differential operator $\mathbf{L} = (\mathbf{D}^3 + \mathbf{D}^2 + \mathbf{I})^2$, and let p be the characteristic polynomial of $\mathbf{L}$.
    a. Use the `factor` command to verify that p has a repeated irreducible quadratic factor over the reals.
    b. Find all solutions of the differential equation $\mathbf{L}(y) = 0$.
    c. Find the solution of the differential equation $\mathbf{L}(y) = e^x$ satisfying the

    initial condition $\mathbf{D}^i(y)(0) = \begin{cases} 1 \text{ if } i = 2 \\ 0 \text{ otherwise} \end{cases}$.

Problems on Differential Equations

Hooke's Law and Harmonic Motion

Over a large portion of their designed travel, many springs are linear: The force required to extend the spring a distance s is a constant multiple of s. The constant of proportionality for the spring is called Hooke's constant, and the equation $F = ks$ is called Hooke's law.

Hooke's Law: $F = ks$

If a mass m is attached to the spring, and $s = s(t)$ is a variable, then by Newton's second law of motion, $F(t) = ms''(t)$.

Newton's Second Law: $F(t) = ms''(t)$

Together, Hooke's law and Newton's second law can be used to explore the motion of a system of weights and springs.

Consider the system pictured in Figure 4-1.

If the weight W is pulled to a distance $s(0)$ below its equilibrium position and released, then equating the force given by Newton's second law with that given by Hooke's law yields the equation

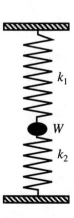

Figure 4-1

$$\frac{w}{g}\frac{d^2s}{dt^2} = -k_1 s(t) + k_2 s(t) - F_d = (k_2 - k_1)s(t) - F_d$$

where

- $s(t)$ is the distance of W from equilibrium position,
- k_1 is Hooke's constant for the upper spring,
- k_2 is Hooke's constant for the lower spring,
- w is the weight of W in pounds,
- g is acceleration due to gravity, and
- F_d is the damping effect of friction.

For simplicity, we assume that the springs are massless.

1. Assuming that $k_1 = 5$, $k_2 = 3$, $g = 32$ ft/sec^2, $s(0) = -12$, $s'(0) = 0$, $w = 17$, and $F_d = 0$, find the function $s(t)$ and plot it over the interval $[0, 6]$.
2. Repeat Problem 1 for $F_d = s'(t)$.

Linear Recurrence Relations[3] and Difference Equations
[rsolve]

The mth-order differential equation

$$a_0 y + a_1 \mathbf{D}(y) + \cdots + a_m \mathbf{D}^m(y) = e^x \qquad (a_m \neq 0)$$

can be rewritten in the form

$$\mathbf{D}^m(y) = b_{m-1} \mathbf{D}^{m-1}(y) + \cdots + b_0 y + e^x,$$

where $b_j = -a_j/a_m$, $j = 0, \ldots, m - 1$. Applying the differential operator $\mathbf{D}^i$ to both sides yields the relation

$$\mathbf{D}^{m+i}(y) = b_{m-1} \mathbf{D}^{m+i-1}(y) + \cdots + b_0 \mathbf{D}^i(y) + e^x$$

which recurs for all integers $i \geq 0$. This is an example of a linear recurrence relation of length m—a fixed linear relation between ith terms of a sequence. In this case, it is the sequence of ith derivatives of the function $y(x)$ and the m terms immediately preceding that. Linear recurrence relations are also called difference equations.

Let S be the vector space of all functions f defined on the nonnegative integers, and let $\mathbf{d}:S \to S$ be the shift operator $\mathbf{d}(f)(n) = f(n + 1)$. Then $\mathbf{d}$ is a linear operator. This is also true of the identity function $\mathbf{I} = \mathbf{d}^0$, the iterates $\mathbf{d}^2 = \mathbf{d} \circ \mathbf{d}$, $\mathbf{d}^3 = \mathbf{d} \circ \mathbf{d} \circ \mathbf{d}$, ..., and all their linear combinations $\mathbf{L} = a_0 \mathbf{I} + a_1 \mathbf{d} + \cdots + a_{m-1} \mathbf{d}^{m-1} + a_m \mathbf{d}^m$, where

$$\begin{aligned} \mathbf{L}(f)(n) &= a_0 f(n) + a_1 \mathbf{d}(f)\,(n) + \cdots + a_m \mathbf{d}^m(f)(n) \\ &= a_0 f(n) + a_1 f(n + 1) + \cdots + a_m f(n + m) \end{aligned}$$

---

[3]For general information on recurrence relations, see, for example, Ronald E. Mickens, *Difference Equations* (New York: Van Nostrand Reinhold, 1990).

In this section, we consider recurrence relations of the form

$$\mathbf{L}(y)(n) = f(n) \tag{4.3.4}$$

where $\mathbf{L}$ is of the form

$$\mathbf{L} = a_0\mathbf{I} + a_1\mathbf{d} + \cdots + a_{m-1}\mathbf{d}^{m-1} + \mathbf{d}^m \tag{4.3.5}$$

Note that, as for all linear transformations, the general solution of the nonhomogeneous equation $\mathbf{L}(y)(n) = f(n)$ is the sum of any particular solution s_p and the general solution s_h of the associated homogeneous equation $\mathbf{L}(y) = 0$. This makes it particularly desirable to find a basis for the solution space of the associated homogeneous equation $\mathbf{L}(y) = 0$ (in other words, for the kernel of $\mathbf{L}$).

A simple illustration is provided by the operator $\mathbf{L} = \mathbf{d} - \mathbf{I}$. Any solution s of $\mathbf{L}(f)(n) = n + 1$ satisfies $s(n) - s(n-1) = n$ or, equivalently, $s(n) = s(n-1) + n$. A solution s_p satisfying the additional equation $s(0) = 0$ is given by $s_p(n) = \sum_{i=0}^{n} i$, which can be easily verified. It is well known that

$$\sum_{i=0}^{n} i = \frac{n(n+1)}{2}.$$ Hence, $s_p(n) = \frac{n(n+1)}{2}$. On the other hand, any solution h of the homogeneous equation $\mathbf{L}(y) = 0$ satisfies $h(n + 1) = h(n)$, and hence is constant. It follows that the general solution s_g of the relation $\mathbf{L}(y)(n) = n$ is given by $s_g(n) = \frac{n(n+1)}{2} + C$, and that all solutions are obtained by varying the parameter C.

The linear operator

$$\mathbf{L} = a_0\mathbf{I} + a_1\mathbf{d} + \cdots + a_{m-1}\mathbf{d}^{m-1} + \mathbf{d}^m$$

is naturally associated with the polynomial

$$p = a_0 + a_1x + \cdots + a_{m-1}x^{m-1} + x^m$$

This polynomial—called the characteristic polynomial of $\mathbf{L}$—is of particular importance in solving the homogeneous equation $\mathbf{L}(y) = 0$. The operator $\mathbf{L}$ is frequently written as $p(\mathbf{d})$; if $p(x)$ has the factorization $p(x) = p_1(x)p_2(x)$, then $\mathbf{L} = p(\mathbf{d})$ has the factorization $\mathbf{L} = p_1(\mathbf{d})p_2(\mathbf{d})$. In particular, if the polynomial $p(x)$ has the factorization

$$p(x) = \prod_{i=1}^{s} (x - r_i)^{e_i} \tag{4.3.6}$$

where $r_i \neq r_j$ if $i \neq j$, then the linear operator $\mathbf{L} = a_0\mathbf{I} + a_1\mathbf{d} + \cdots + a_n\mathbf{d}^m$ has

the factorization $\mathbf{L} = \displaystyle\prod_{i=1}^{s} (\mathbf{d} - r_i\mathbf{I})^{e_i}$.

The solutions of the homogeneous equation $\mathbf{L}(y) = 0$ can be found by solving the s homogeneous equations $(\mathbf{d} - r_i\mathbf{I})^{e_i}(y) = 0$. The solutions of the equation $\mathbf{L}(y) = 0$ are linear combinations of the solutions of the homogeneous equations $(\mathbf{d} - r_i\mathbf{I})^{e_i}(y) = 0$.

It is easy to see that the solutions of $(\mathbf{d} - k\mathbf{I})(f) = 0$—that is, of $f(n + 1) = kf(n)$—are completely determined by the value $f(0)$. In fact, $f(1) = kf(0)$, $f(2) = kf(1) = k^2 f(0)$, ..., and $f(n) = kf(n - 1) = k^n f(0)$); therefore the general solution s_h is given by $s_h(n) = Ck^n$. Hence, if $e_i = 1$ for all i in Equation (4.3.6), then the solutions of the difference equation $\mathbf{L}(y) = 0$ are the linear combinations $f(n) = C_1 r_1^n + C_2 r_2^n + \cdots + C_m r_m^n$, of the solutions $f_i(n) = r_i^n$, of the r equations $(\mathbf{d} - r_i\mathbf{I})(y) = 0$.

You can solve many recurrence equations in *Maple* with the `rsolve` command. The **d** notation is not supported; *Maple* uses $f(n + i)$ for $\mathbf{d}^i(f)(n)$. Consider the example $\mathbf{L} = \mathbf{d}^2 - 4\mathbf{d} + 3\mathbf{I} = (\mathbf{d} - \mathbf{I})(\mathbf{d} - 3\mathbf{I})$. Here, it is easiest to treat the expression as a polynomial.

Let $\mathbf{L} = \mathbf{d}^2 - 4\mathbf{d} + 3\mathbf{I}$ *be the operator.*

- `L:=d^2-4*d+3;`
It is convenient and customary to write k for $k\mathbf{I}$.

This sets up the recurrence relation $\mathbf{L}(y) = 0$ *in Maple notation.*

- `i:='i';`
- `REQ:=`
  » `sum(coeff(L,d,i)*f(n+i),i=0..2)=0;`
This gives the desired form $3f(n) - 4f(n + 1) + f(n + 2) = 0$.

Use `rsolve` *to solve the equations.*

- `rs[h]:=rsolve(REQ,f);`[4]
You can solve for either f or $f(n)$; the result is the same.

This shows that $\mathbf{rs}_h$ *is a linear combination of the solutions of* $(\mathbf{d} - \mathbf{I})(y) = 0$ *and* $(\mathbf{d} - 3\mathbf{I})(y) = 0$.

- `rsolve(g(n+1)-g(n)=0,g);`
- `rsolve(f(n+1)-3*f(n)=0,f);`
The solution of the first equation is a multiple of the function $\mathbf{I}(n) = n$; the solution of the second is a multiple of the function $f(n) = 3^n$. If you get an error message in either case, you may be using an assigned variable.

Now consider the difference equation $\mathbf{L}(y)(n) = n^2$, where $\mathbf{L}(y) = \mathbf{d}^2 - 4\mathbf{d} + 3$.

Use `rsolve` *to obtain the general solution.*

- `rs[g]:=`
- `rsolve(f(n+2)-4*f(n+1)+3*f(n)=n^2,f);`
The solution is completely general: All solutions are obtained by varying the parameters $f(0)$, and $f(1)$ in the general solution $\mathbf{rs}_g$.

---

[4]I have found that the notation *rs[h]*, *rs[g]* , and *rs[p]* works better with `rsolve` than the notation *s[h]*, *s[g]*, *rs[p]* in the original release of *Maple V*, but I have been unable to determine a reason for this. The definition of *s[g]* sometimes destroys the definition of *s[h]*.

You can obtain particular
solutions using subs .

- rs[p]:=subs(f(0)=0,f(1)=0,rs[g]);
All solutions are obtained by varying the constants.

You can verify the relation
$rs_g = rs_p + rs_h$.

- rs[p]+rs[h];
- rs[g];
The two should be the same (except, perhaps, for their form).

The Casoratian

It is a theorem of difference equations that the kernel of a linear operator of the form

$$\mathbf{L} = a_0\mathbf{I} + a_1\mathbf{d} + \cdots + \mathbf{d}^m$$

is an m-dimensional vector space. The Casoratian function gives you a means of verifying that you have all the solutions; its use is analogous to the use of the Wronskian function for differential equations.

$$\text{Let } \mathbf{L} = \prod_{i=2}^{6} (\mathbf{d} - i\mathbf{I}), \text{ so that the solution space of } \mathbf{L}(y) = 0 \text{ has dimen-}$$

sion five.

Define the recurrence
relation $\mathbf{L}(y) = 0$.

- i:='i';
- product((d-i),i=2..6);
- L:=expand(");

- REQ:=
» sum(coeff(L,d,i)*f(n+i),i=0..5)=0;

Solve the recurrence
equation with rsolve.

- i:='i';
- rs[h]:=rsolve(REQ,f);
Notice that the solutions are all linear combinations of the functions $g_j(n) = j^n, j = 2...6$.

This shows that every linear
combination of the functions
$g_j(n) = j^n, j = 2...6, is a$
solution.

- for i from 2 to 6
» do
»   c.i:=coeff(rs[h],i^n)
» od;

- M:=
» genmatrix([c2,c3,c4,c5,c6],
» [f(0),f(1),f(2),f(3),f(4)]);
- det(");
Notice that M is the matrix of coefficients of $f(0), ..., f(4)$. This shows that by a suitable choice of $f(0), ..., f(4)$, every linear combination of $g_2, ..., g_6$ can be obtained; in particular, $g_j = j^n$ is a linear combination of the form indicated in rs_h.

Note that if $k_2g_2 + \cdots + k_6g_6 = 0$ then also $\mathbf{d}^i(k_2g_2 + \cdots + k_6g_6) = k_2\mathbf{d}^i(g_2) + \cdots + k_6\mathbf{d}^i(g_6) = 0$, $i = 1, 2, \ldots$. If this is the case, then the vectors $\mathbf{v}_j(n) = (g_j(n), g_j(n + 1), \ldots, g_j(n + 4))$ satisfy the relation $k_2\mathbf{v}_2(n) + \cdots + k_6\mathbf{v}_6(n) = 0$. This implies that the matrix $K(n) = [\mathbf{v}_2(n), \ldots, \mathbf{v}_6(n)]$ is singular for all n.

The matrix $K(n)$ is called the Casoratian matrix of the functions $n \rightarrow j^n$; the determinant $\mathbf{C}(n) = \det(K(n))$ is called the Casoratian or Casorati determinant.

This defines the generating function for the Casoratian matrix.

• g:=(i,j)->(j+1)^(i-1);

This bears some similarity to a generating function for a Vandermonde matrix.

This generates the Casoratian matrix.

• K:=matrix(6,6,g);

If the functions f_j, $j = 2\ldots6$ are linearly dependent, then so are the columns of this matrix.

The determinant shows that the columns of K are linearly independent, and therefore that the solutions $g_2, \ldots, g_6$ are a basis for $\mathbf{rs}_h$.

• det(K);

The matrix K is the transpose of a Vandermonde matrix, so its determinant is nonzero.

Initial Conditions

It is a theorem that, for any difference operator

$$L = a_0I + a_1d + \cdots + a_{m-1}\mathbf{d}^{m-1} + \mathbf{d}^m$$

each vector $\mathbf{v} = (v_1, v_2, \ldots, v_m)$ in $\Re^m$ corresponds to a unique solution f satisfying $f(i) = v_{i+1}$, $i = 0\ldots m - 1$. In fact, it is obvious that the values $f(i)$, $\ldots, f(i + m - 1)$ determine $f(m + i)$ and that the choice of $f(0), \ldots, f(m - 1)$ can be made arbitrarily. Consider the operator $L = \mathbf{d}^4 + 4\mathbf{d}^3 - 3\mathbf{d}^2 + 2\mathbf{d} - 1$. If initial values $f(0), f(1), f(2)$, and $f(3)$ are chosen, and $\mathbf{L}(f) = 0$, then $f(n + 4) = -4f(n + 3) + 3f(n + 2) - 2f(n + 1) + f(n)$, for all $n = 0, 1, \ldots$. For example, assume $f(i) = i$, $i = 0\ldots3$.

This procedure will calculate $f(n)$ for any n.

```
• f:=proc(n)
»    if 0<=n and n<=3 then n
»      else -4*f(n-1)+3*f(n-2)-
»        2*f(n-3)+f(n-4)
»    fi;
» end;
```

This shows the first twenty-five values.

• for i from 0 to 24 do f(i) od;

If this runs slowly, you can speed it up by following the line f:=proc(n) with the line option remember;.

The correspondence between $\mathbf{v} = (v_1, v_2, \ldots, v_m)$ in $\Re^m$ and the function f defined by $f(i) = v_{i+1}$, $i = 0\ldots m-1$ is also linear, so all solutions of the homogeneous equation $\mathbf{L}(y) = 0$ can be found from any m solutions $\{f_i\}_{i=1}^m$ that correspond to a basis for $\Re^m$.

Earlier you found the basic solutions $g_j(n) = j^n$ of the recurrence rela-

tion $\mathbf{L}(f) = 0$ for $\mathbf{L} = \prod_{j=2}^{6} (\mathbf{d} - j\mathbf{I})$. This basis for s_h corresponds to the basis

$\mathbf{u}_1 = (1,2,4,8,16)$, $\mathbf{u}_2 = (1,3,9,27,81)$, $\mathbf{u}_3 = (1,4,16,64,256)$, $\mathbf{u}_4 = (1,5,25,125,625)$, $\mathbf{u}_5 = (1,6,36,216,1296)$ for $\Re^5$. In the following, you will find the solution $\mathbf{h}_1$ of $\mathbf{L}(y) = 0$ corresponding to the vector $\mathbf{e}_1 = (1,0,0,0,0)$.

Define the functions g_j.

- `g[2]:=n->2^n;`
- `g[3]:=n->3^n;`
- `g[4]:=n->4^n;`
- `g[5]:=n->5^n;`
- `g[6]:=n->6^n;`

Put the solutions $g_j = j^n$ into a vector.

- `b:=vector([seq(g[j],j=2..6)]);`

Define the vector $\mathbf{e}_1 = (1,0,0,0,0)$.

- `e[1]:=vector([1,0,0,0,0]);`

Define the matrix $M = [\mathbf{u}_1,\mathbf{u}_2,\mathbf{u}_3,\mathbf{u}_4,\mathbf{u}_5]$.

- `vandermonde([2,3,4,5,6]);`
- `M:=transpose(");`

The $\mathbf{u}_i$ are the column vectors of M.

Solve the equation $M\mathbf{x} = \mathbf{e}_1$.

- `rref(augment(M,e[1]));`
- `a:=backsub(");`

Note that $\mathbf{a}$ is the coefficient vector of $\mathbf{e}_1$ with respect to the column vectors of M.

Compute the solution $\mathbf{h}_1 = \langle \mathbf{b},\mathbf{a}\rangle$ corresponding to $\mathbf{e}_1$.

- `h[1]:=innerprod(b,a);`

Recall that $\mathbf{b} = (g_2, g_3, g_4, g_5, g_6)$ is the vector of basic solutions of $\mathbf{L}(y) = 0$.

The solution $\mathbf{h}_1$ should now correspond to the vector $\mathbf{e}_1$.

- `for j from 0 to 4`
- `» do`
- `»   h[1](j)`
- `» od;`

The function $\mathbf{h}[1]$ should satisfy $\mathbf{h}_1(j) = \delta_{0j}$, $j = 0\ldots 4$.

You can also solve initial condition problems directly with `rsolve`, as demonstrated in the following, which assumes that f is undefined and that the definition of **REQ** is still active.

You may want to verify that
f is unassigned and that
REQ has the desired value.

- `f:='f';`
- `REQ;`

If the response to REQ that you get is different from

$$-720\ y(n) + 1044\ y(n+1) -$$
$$580\ y(n+2) + 155\ y(n+3)$$
$$-20\ y(n+4) + y(n+5) = 0$$

then you will need to reassign REQ.

This obtains the solution
corresponding to $\mathbf{e}_1 =$
(1,0,0,0,0).

- `rsolve({REQ,f(0)=1,f(1)=0,`
- `» f(2)=0,f(3)=0,f(4)=0},f);`

Exercises on Linear Recurrence Relations

1. The sum of the first n positive integers is described by the non-homogeneous recursion relation $s(n+1) - s(n) = n+1$ with the initial condition $s(0) = 0$. A similar recursion relation describes the sum of the mth powers of the first n positive integers. Use `rsolve` to find formulas for the following sums (such formulas are traditionally written in factored form).

    a. $\displaystyle\sum_{i=1}^{n} i^4$ b. $\displaystyle\sum_{i=1}^{n} i^5$ c. $\displaystyle\sum_{i=1}^{n} i^7$

2. Use the results of Exercise 7 to form a conjecture about the nature of the functions $s_m(n) = \displaystyle\sum_{i=1}^{n} i^m$. Test your conjecture for $m = 10$ and $m = 15$.

3. Assume $\mathbf{F} = \mathbf{d} - 2\mathbf{I}$, and $\mathbf{L} = \mathbf{F} \circ \mathbf{F} \circ \mathbf{F}$.
    a. Show that 2^n, $n2^n$, and $n^2 2^n$ are solutions of $\mathbf{L}(f) = 0$.
    b. Show that the three solutions in part a are linearly independent. Can you conclude that they are a basis for the kernel of $\mathbf{L}$?
    c. What can you conjecture about the solutions of $(\mathbf{D} - r)^f$ in general? Verify your conjecture for $\mathbf{F} \circ \mathbf{F} \circ \mathbf{F} \circ \mathbf{F} \circ \mathbf{F}$.

4. If the characteristic polynomial $C(x)$ of a difference operator $\mathbf{L}$ has a complex root, then the factorization of $C(x)$ over the reals has an irreducible real quadratic factor $((x + a)^2 + b^2)$. Let $\mathbf{L}$ be the linear operator $\mathbf{L} = ((\mathbf{d} + 2\mathbf{I})^2 + (3^2 + 2^2)\mathbf{I})$. Use `rsolve`, `evalc`, and `simplify` to determine the form of the solution of the recurrence equation $\mathbf{L}(f) = 0$.

Problems on Linear Recurrence Relations

1. A famous problem (known as "The Problem of the Towers of Hanoi") involves sixty-four disks with holes in their centers stacked on one of three poles. The disks are arranged so that the largest is on the bottom of

the stack, then the next largest, and so on. The problem is to move the disks to another of the three poles—one disk at a time—without ever placing a larger disk on top of a smaller one. You may have seen smaller versions of this problem as children's puzzles.

   a. Determine the minimum number of moves required to solve the problem for n disks.

   b. Determine the minimum length of time (in years) required to solve the problem for sixty-four disks, if the disks were moved at the rate of one per second.

2. A variation of the "Towers" problem has the three poles in a row, and the disks on one end. In this version a second condition is imposed: Disks can be moved only to an adjacent pole.

   a. Determine the minimum number of moves required to solve this version for n disks.

   b. Determine the minimum length of time (in years) required to solve this version of the problem for sixty-four disks, if the disks were moved at the rate of one per second.

3. The following famous problem originated with Leonardo de Pisa (also known as Fibonacci), the most important mathematician of the thirteenth century.

   Assume that a farmer acquires n_0 pairs of newborn rabbits. Assume also that each pair gives birth to one additional pair at the end of every month, beginning with the second month, and that all their descendants do the same.

   a. Assuming that none of the rabbits dies, how many rabbits are there after n months?

   b. How many rabbits does the farmer have at the end of ten years if he begins with exactly one pair?

Index

(*Maple* commands are shown in `Courier` type.)